794.342

5/12	DATE DUE		

Munchkin Tennis

A Parent's Guide to Teaching Tennis Fundamentals

By the United States Professional Tennis Registry

TRIUMPH BOOKS
Chicago

ACKNOWLEDGEMENTS

Many people contributed to Munchkin Tennis. Their experiences with thousands of young children in tennis helped make this book a valuable addition to tennis. They included: Jim Brown, Colleen Cosgrove, Leif Dahlgren, Anneke Jelsma-de Jong, Steve Milano, Teresa Phillips, John Weil and Marceil Whitney. Thanks very much.

In particular, Gregg Presuto deserves special recognition for donating to the USPTR his file of activities and games, his professional contributions from the field of psychology and his personal insight into and experiences in tennis with young children.

Copyrighted material from *Beyond X's and O's* by Jack Hutslar; *Improving Relationship Skills in Youth Sport Coaches* by Frank L. Smoll and Ronald E. Smith.

Illustrations by Ralph Sutton.

Dennis Van der Meer, President & Founder
U.S. Professional Tennis Registry
Hilton Head Island, South Carolina
April 1993

THE USPTR

The USPTR was established in 1976 to certify tennis teachers through an internationally-recognized test based on a standardized teaching method. Development of this method began when Dennis Van der Meer and Billie Jean King began a tennis camp in 1972, and saw a need for an introductory method to teaching.

While most tennis experts agree that though there are many different ways to teach tennis, the concept of a worldwide teaching standard is sound. In today's transient, extremely mobile society, tennis players should be able to continue to develop their basic skills without being subject to the whims of each individual pro.

Today, the USPTR boasts more than 7,000 tennis teachers in more than 100 countries who are certified to teach tennis using a biomechanically-sound method.

In order to become certified by the USPTR, a written and on-court examination must be taken. The written portion covers knowledge of tactics and strategy, as well as teaching and corrective techniques. The on-court tests examine the ability of the instructor to demonstrate strokes and to conduct a class in a real teaching situation. In the skills test, ball control, placement, and specialty shot execution must be demonstrated. In the teaching test, the instructor must teach a group and a private lesson.

The highest rating, that of Professional, is achieved when the applicant scores a Professional rating on each of the three portions of the certification test: written, skills and teaching. A lesser rating on any portion of the test may qualify the applicant for an Instructor or Associate Instructor rating.

Applicants may attempt to upgrade their rating after a 30-day waiting period. USPTR Tennis Teacher Workshops are held in the U.S. and Internationally. Certification sites and testers are located around the world.

International Standard Book Number: 1-880141-40-X

For more information on the USPTR, contact:

United States Professional Tennis Registry
P.O. Box 4739
Hilton Head Island, South Carolina 29938
(800) 421-6289 or (803) 785-7244
Fax: (803) 686-2033

This book is available in quantity at special discounts for
your group or organization. For further information, contact:

Triumph Books
644 South Clark Street, Suite 2000
Chicago, Illinois 60605
(312) 939-3330
Fax: (312) 663-3557

Written by Jack Hutslar, Ph.D.
Cover design by Sam Concialdi
Typography and design by Jeff Dalpiaz

Printed in the United States of America

Library of Congress Cataloging-in-Publication Data
Munchkin Tennis: a parent's guide to teaching tennis funda-
mentals / by the United States Professional Tennis Registry.
      p.   cm.
   ISBN 1-880141-40-X : $14.95
   1. Tennis for children.   I. United States Professional
Tennis Registry
GV1001.4.C45M86   1993   93-7916
796.342'08'3 — dc20   CIP

TABLE OF CONTENTS

1 Introduction to Munchkin Tennis   1

2 About Children   9

3 Self-help Teaching Skills   19

4 Basic Skills of Munchkin Tennis   43

5 Munchkin I: Movement Education, Juggling and Tennis Tasks   57

6 Munchkin II: Low Organized Games   79

7 Munchkin III: Tennis Lead-up Games   217

8 Munchkin IV: Graduated Tennis Method   241

9 Programs in Action   249

10 How to Start Munchkin Tennis   277

Bibliography   295

Index   299

CHAPTER 1

INTRODUCTION TO MUNCHKIN TENNIS

Tennis is a lifetime sport from which all age groups find personal enjoyment, opportunities to mix with others socially, as well as the health benefits of vigorous exercise. In today's society, this means cradle to grave opportunities. As in the past, concerned parents assume a great deal of the responsibility for what their children learn. Unlike the past, sport has taken a more central position in the lives of many more adults. Parents who play sports like tennis want their children to play tennis and enjoy it as they do. However, the good intentions of parents can turn into work or punishment for children.

The purpose of Munchkin Tennis is to show parents how they can expose their young children, ages three or four to nine, to the skills of tennis so that it is fun and enjoyable for both. In this way, your children may continue to play the sport as they grow up. This is not to say that your Munchkins will become world class players when you get them started early. Too many factors come into play to make that pronouncement. Just be satisfied that they can play tennis throughout their lives, possibly with you in a host of singles and doubles adventures, and have fun doing it.

In time, parents who introduce tennis to their children through the hundreds of activities presented in Munchkin Tennis may find themselves teaching tennis to others. Parents may find new students from among your friends, your children's friends or other children from the courts where you play. With that possibility in mind, Munchkin Tennis provides sufficient information to help parents get a good start on becoming teaching pros, if that becomes a goal.

Munchkin Tennis provides introductory movement and ball skills, activities and tennis games for children age nine and under. It is based on fun-filled movements and games, not repetitive drills.

Tennis for young children is not a new idea. A game of "small" tennis using short wooden paddles and court was demonstrated by Dennis Van der Meer and Jaro Houba in 1955. Houba, a tennis coach, was one of the innovators of this form of tennis in Czechoslovakia.

The acquisition of tennis skills by young children can be important in their future involvement in tennis. Therefore, it is crucial that their current experience in tennis be very positive. Delayed gratification is not in their thoughts. Enjoyment must occur now, not later. The cornerstone of Munchkin Tennis is to have fun now learning some of the basics of the game.

Model for Munchkin Tennis

The model or theoretical framework for Munchkin Tennis is built on three concepts. They are people, tennis, and a philosophy. More specifically, they are:

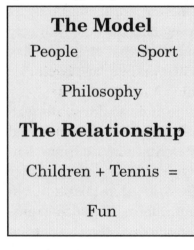

The Model

People   Sport

Philosophy

The Relationship

Children + Tennis =

Fun

(1) young children; their inherent biological, psychological and social characteristics; and the relationships they develop with tennis now and in the future;

(2) the sport of tennis, its skills and knowledge, and space or court; and

(3) a philosophy of working with children including formal and informal methods of instruction used by parents and other teachers that are rooted in fun.

The idea for Munchkin Tennis has been around for quite some time.

People. Munchkin Tennis revolves around children and various other instructors. However, the most important people in the lives of most children in the nine and under age group are parents. Mothers, in particular, are the parent most likely to be involved with their young children in tennis. They are the ones who make sure youngsters are signed up, ready to go, haul Munchkins here and there, buy their clothes and rackets, nurse their wounds, and applaud their achievements.

Brothers, sisters and neighborhood friends are also significant figures in the lives of children of all ages. In fact, children enroll in all types of programs to be with friends. Siblings are often enrolled in programs together to: (1) see that they acquire new skills to broaden their development, (2) give parents a break, or (3) see that one does not get more than the other to keep peace in the family.

Parents and teachers are important. They can play a central role in the lives of young children. Children like and admire adults who pay attention to them and treat them well. They can become quite attached to their teachers, whether in the classroom or on the tennis courts.

On the courts, Munchkin Tennis revolves around children, partners, parents, and instructors. Young children, as with teens, young singles and senior citizens, have characteristics that set them apart from other age groups. Parents may be familiar with their own children. They can be even more effective teachers when

they know the range of characteristics and limitations of the age groups with which they work.

For instance, Munchkins are very egocentric. Me first, is quite normal. Getting their turn and playing fair are two of their major concerns.

Another characteristic is that youngsters vary tremendously in the rate at which they learn new skills. Initially, some may have poor hand-eye coordination. They see friends making contact with the ball easily and wonder why they miss repeatedly. In seeing this, parents can help them with extra turns, be more precise with tosses, or provide extra encouragement when signs of frustration or disinterest appear. See Chapter 2 for more information about the characteristics of children.

Friends on the courts can be partners and opponents, depending on the activity. Being on the same side as a friend can make or break the whole day. In fact, friendships may be more important than tennis. When players become older and more skillful, tennis may assume first priority. Then friendships begin to develop from within tennis.

There is one major point to be gained from this portion of the model. It is this. Personal relationships among people, not skill development, dominate Munchkin Tennis. Establish proper relationships and all else will follow.

Tennis, the sport. Tennis is not a driving force among children when compared to hunger, fatigue, friends, cartoon shows and the right toys. Tennis is merely an opportunity. That is, some children will have the opportunity to play tennis and others will not. It is uncommon for parents to go out of their way to see that their children have tennis lessons, at least compared to going to camp, the right school, or purchasing the right toys.

In time, tennis may become important. This can occur when children: (1) live near tennis courts, (2) learn from friendly instructors who know their stuff, and (3) do well and have success.

Beginning tennis players of all ages must learn the basics. For beginners beyond the Munchkin years, the basic skills are forehand, backhand, serve and volley. They represent the physical or psycho-motor domain.

For Munchkins, the basic skills are learning to handle the racket and the ball, making contact with the ball, controlling the ball, moving to hit the ball, and hitting the ball to a target or partner. Eventually, they learn to play so an opponent cannot return it successfully.

Tennis players, as in any sport, must learn the cognitive aspects of the game. This is knowledge and includes the court, rules, etiquette, scoring, strategies, opponents, equipment, social matches, and serious tournaments. Some youngsters will be eager to learn so they can advance to the next higher level of play.

When their skill level improves, they will play more skillful opponents and adopt attitudes and values unique to sports, tennis specifically. Attitudes and values are referred to as the affective domain. They will work to improve their skills, train hard, and assign greater value to winning than losing. As Munchkins, however, their concerns are hitting the ball, keeping the ball inside the correct lines, and doing well in fun-filled tennis activities and games. This will help them learn new skills but it is generally not something for which they are striving. In short, Munchkins just want to have fun. Thanks to you, it happens to be tennis fun.

There is a major point to be clarified in this portion of the model. It is this. Tennis is a sport that some children learn easily and enjoy playing. Yet, few will embrace tennis as a central life interest to rival friends and family. Some Munchkins may try tennis just once. Some will play once and not try again for several years. Whatever the initial experience, it should be enjoyable, produce good memories, and provide a few skills to build on in the future.

The philosophy. The philosophy of Munchkin Tennis is reflected in how parents and instructors teach, and how they treat their children. The overriding philosophy or goal for children in Munchkin Tennis is that it be fun, F-U-N, fun.

Having fun is the best way of keeping Munchkins interested in the program.

The second goal is that activities be organized around total participation. Playing is far better than not playing. Total participation is the core of skill acquisition, and that is fun.

The third goal is to learn the basic skills of tennis. In Munchkin Tennis, this is done through fun-filled games and activities. Children like games and they come back to repeat what they like.

Parents should expect the acquisition of tennis skills by young children to be a slow but enjoyable learning process. Munchkins may take two or three years to learn skills that children over the age of nine or 10 learn in one series of lessons.

Safety is an important goal in all sport and recreation programs today. Children who are unfamiliar with tennis rackets and balls, particularly children with little self-control, may use rackets as bats, axes and swords. They may also hit balls wildly without concern for the consequences or the safety of others. Take time to teach players about these hazards. Teach them the proper skills of tennis. Be present when children are in your care, and purchase

accident and liability insurance to cover yourself.

Balance is a goal that needs renewed attention. It has several facets. First, in tennis, it means that children should be well rounded in all aspects of the game. Second, children should have experiences in other sports. Third, children need to do well in school, and participate in non-sport activities like music and computer technology. In particular, children must do well in math and language, both reading and writing. Well-rounded children who acquire the basic skills of life have the potential to become good, if not great, at many things.

Finally, parents should conduct Munchkin Tennis in a positive, supportive atmosphere. Youngsters make a variety of mistakes. This is one of the main characteristics of beginners. Rather than dwell on errors, introduce new skills and repeatedly tell them what they are doing right.

For instance, a child might take a very good stroke but miss the ball. Despite this obvious error, find something positive to say about the stroke. It might be: "You did everything right but just missed the ball. Watch the ball hit your racket." It might also be: "You had your side to the net just right that time."

Do not be negative or critical. Be encouraging! Tell them what they are doing right even when they do not contact the ball at the correct moment or miss it completely. Be positive.

The philosophy of Munchkin Tennis involves fun, total participation, learning the basic skills, safety and balance. It was adapted with permission from *Beyond X's and O's* by Jack Hutslar. (See bibliography)

Munchkin Tennis
The book . . .

The remaining chapters of Munchkin Tennis present material to help parents develop and conduct well-rounded programs for their own children and others. Chapter 2 reviews the basic characteristics of children and how they differ from other age groups. We sometimes think that all children are like our children. For better or worse, this is usually not the case.

Chapter 3 covers basic skills of teaching and coaching, plus the psychology of coaching and teaching. It includes useful self-help material for parents who do not have a formal background in education. At the same time, teachers and coaches who have not worked with young children in tennis will find this chapter helpful.

Chapters 4, 5, 6, 7 and 8 present the basic skills of tennis. They describe how children can learn tennis in fun, exciting and vigorous ways. These five chapters contain an encyclopedia of activities and games from which parents can select and design their own program of Munchkin Tennis.

Chapter 9 provides an in-depth look at several tennis programs for young children. Chapter 10 concludes with suggestions for starting your own formal or informal Munchkin Tennis program. It includes staff training, planning, reduced-size equipment, tips for making programs work, marketing and advertising, preparing parents and a bibliography. The Index is found on the last five pages of Munchkin Tennis.

Summary

There are three major considerations about sport for young children. They are people, the essential skills of the sport itself, and a guiding philosophy. In the case of Munchkin Tennis, it is good to remind yourself regularly that you are dealing with young children, not highly motivated teens or adults, and very elementary ball and racket skills. Then, keep reminding yourself that the relationship between tennis, Munchkin Tennis, and children is based on a philosophy that emphasizes fun.

The core of Munchkin Tennis is to have fun learning the basic skills of tennis. Children should have fun learning and playing tennis. Parents should have fun teaching Munchkins how to play tennis. Parents should have fun playing tennis with Munchkins. When parents have fun, it is a good sign your Munchkins are having fun too.

CHAPTER 2

ABOUT CHILDREN

Young children, Munchkins, are unlike other beginning tennis players. Most older children are able to focus fairly well on the tennis skills they are to learn. Very young children may be consumed by airplanes, flashy cars, noisy trucks, butterflies, bugs, hair braids, and cartwheels.

Children are not miniature adults nor should they be treated as adults. They are immature physically, mentally and socially compared to adults, young adults, or teenagers.

Children can play tennis with equipment of all shapes and sizes.

For instance, the ratio of body mass to skin surface is less for children than adults. In hot and humid environments, children lose body fluids through evaporation faster than adults. As a result, children require more water than adults. Munchkins need frequent water and shade breaks, about every 15 minutes or so.

It is common for young children, particularly girls, to have neither played with balls nor engaged in a wide range of physical

activities. As a consequence, things active children do easily and parents take for granted may be novel experiences for other children. Throwing and catching is second nature for some, new for others. Children who participate in a variety of play and sport activities are usually strong and move easily.

Sedentary beginners have yet to feel the joy of rapid and sustained movement, physical exertion, and "warm" court temperatures. Their development as tennis players will hinge on having a good time or making satisfactory progress. Factors that keep their interest in tennis are the personal relationships on the court, the personality and positive teaching methods of the parent, and a supportive but non-threatening atmosphere.

Essential Characteristics. The essential characteristics of all sports are strength, speed, endurance, power, agility or quickness, balance and flexibility. Tennis skills such as ball judgment are covered in Chapter 4, Basic Skills of Munchkin Tennis.

Strength is important. It is needed to maintain a proper grip on the racket, hold the racket parallel to the ground, make contact with the ball at the proper time, and stroke through the ball. Agility is the ability to move quickly from one position to another. It determines how well children are able to move to the ball and get into position for strokes. Speed becomes important later when they play tennis games against others over a large area. Children with limited activity backgrounds can make substantial improvements in strength, speed and agility as they spend more time in tennis activities.

Lessons to be learned from this by parents and coaches are threefold:

(1) Starting tennis at an early age does not necessarily guaran tee future success as tennis players.

(2) Well skilled children do not necessarily become the most highly skilled teenage and adult tennis players.

(3) Comparatively unskilled children may become highly skilled teenage and adult tennis players.

Transfer of training. Many children participate in a variety of activities. Similarities between the skills of other activities and tennis can influence how rapidly new skills are learned. For instance, the foot position used to hit a baseball, golf ball and tennis ball are similar. Yet, the swings are different. The grip for badminton, racquetball and tennis are similar, but tennis requires a relatively fixed wrist. Other racket sports use a wrist snap. Parents can see where both positive and negative transfer of training occurs in these examples.

Participating in other sports is also a key component of Munchkin Tennis.

Children may experience some difficulty shifting from other sport activities to tennis. For instance, youngsters who have played baseball and softball have ample practice with hand-eye coordination and spatial relationships in catching and batting. At the same time, they may have difficulty slowing down a forceful baseball swing to make a controlled tennis stroke.

In their minds, the objective of tennis may be to hit the ball over the fence surrounding the tennis courts. This is referred to as negative transfer of training. Certain games (See Chapters 5, 6 and 7) help teach children that tennis is a game that involves "placing" the ball with controlled strokes, not power.

Positive transfer of training is most evident where children are able to make contact with tennis balls repeatedly as a result of previous experiences in other ball sports. This is apparent in the "ups and downs" used to develop racket control, forehand and backhand strokes, and the overhand throwing pattern used in serving.

Hand-eye coordination. Tennis relies on hand-eye coordination and positioning the body properly in relation to the ball. Hand-eye coordination is the ability to bounce and catch tennis balls, toss and catch with a partner, toss the ball up to serve, and the coordinated action needed to bring racket and ball together in "ups and downs" and strokes. It is quite evident that some children, even adults, have very poorer hand-eye coordination compared to others. Stroke after stroke results in miss after miss. Just making contact becomes a reason to celebrate. Young children probably do not understand why they miss the ball when others make contact so easily.

Hitting a sponge ball with a coat hanger racket helps children develop hand-eye coordination.

Spatial orientation problems seem to accompany hand-eye problems. Many children seem also to have difficulty judging where to position their body and racket in relation to the ball. That is, they may be in the wrong place more than the right place when preparing to stroke the ball. The result is another miss.

These attributes are not related to body build, obesity, fitness level or lack of experience. Fortunately, some improvement occurs with practice.

Parents can help these children by spending more fun-filled time on the courts with these children hitting tennis balls. Children with hand-eye and spatial relations problems improve with extra attention and practice time on the courts.

For older children, even teenagers, poor hand-eye coordination and spatial relations problems can be explained as one might explain eye color, freckles, height or body build. Some have it. Some do not. Their plight is that, compared to others, they must work very hard to make a little progress. The same thing happens in math and music.

All Munchkin Tennis instructors should toss the ball so each player can easily hit it.

Parents of children with late hand-eye and spatial relationship development have two options. They can help them understand and be satisfied with slow development as a tennis player. At the same time, they can provide them with opportunities to try other sports like archery, bowling, dance, golf, gymnastics, running or swimming. These sports do not involve rapid movement to hit a moving object.

However, discontinuing tennis should be a decision for players to make, not parents and not coaches. Furthermore, this decision need not be made at all, and certainly not after a session or two of Munchkin Tennis.

Tracking. Tracking a tennis ball is difficult for young children. Tracking problems may appear similar to the hand-eye and spatial relations problem just noted. However, it is encouraging to learn that the ability to track objects improves dramatically with age.

Tracking tennis balls, the ability to predict where they will land, and hitting high bouncing tennis balls are readiness problems. Like walking, talking, and time, they are not innate life-long deficiencies.

Young children can track balls more easily when the trajectory is flat or low at a slow speed. They have great difficulty tracking high trajectory bounces like moon balls, lobs and overheads. As youngsters get older, they can find a ball in the air, determine the path of a ball, predict about where the ball will land, and decide whether they need to move in, to either side or back to hit it. Tracking improves automatically with age.

Hand-eye coordination, spatial relationships and tracking are three kinesthetic elements in tennis over which parents have some control. Most children can hit the tennis ball when they see the ball, know the ball is coming, and it is fed to them slowly with a low bounce. When the speed of the ball is increased, their swing speed tends also to increase. Precision decreases as does control. Keep the ball low and slow to foster success.

Parents can help players make contact with the ball in two other ways. They should know the individual characteristics of the children. Use this knowledge to toss the ball to the spot where the player will swing. In fact, parents should try to hit each child's racket with each toss. When children hit the ball, they have fun.

Later, beginners will play tennis games as well as matches against other players with the parent feeding balls. In these situations, it is helpful if children are permitted to play the ball on one, two and even three bounces.

Other important characteristics. There are more similarities than differences between young boys and girls. Boys tend to be more active and aggressive, girls more passive and compliant. It is common for children, and some adults, to have short attention spans. As attention wanes, disturbances increase. These unsettling conditions can be kept to a minimum when parents plan a variety of activities and short "lectures" of one or two minutes. Keep activity time high.

Children are very egocentric. Me first is quite normal. Getting their turn and being fair are primary concerns. Children in particular, seek adult recognition and approval. Some are forever asking instructors to "watch this."

Emotions are fragile but they change rapidly from crying to laughing. Unlike adults, they quickly forget scoldings and do not hold grudges.

Most younger children do not pace themselves. They go 100 percent all of the time. Therefore, frequent changes of pace and rest periods are needed to prevent overexertion. This sustains energy levels and enthusiasm.

Younger children are quite dependent on adult leadership. They do not work well on their own. Even with good planning and preparation, Munchkins still need close supervision and direct guidance. Small groups of one parent to two to four players (eight if necessary) on one court produce the best results.

Fortunately, children adapt to nearly any system or style of teaching. As with most children, they are eager to learn, but the progress of Munchkins is much slower than that of children age 10 and older. Yet, some still learn faster than others. In fact, one or two in nearly every group may be heads and shoulders above the others.

Wins and losses are unimportant and quickly forgotten by most young children. However, a few will be very competitive. They play as if life ends when they do not win. Losses leave them in tears while wins bring Olympian bursts of joy. These youngsters usually bring their winning attitude (i.e., winning is the only thing) to tennis from older family members.

Parents can reduce their focus on winning in several ways. Move quickly from one activity to the next. Do not attach great importance to winning and losing games. Do not single out winners for special praise. Acknowledge it and move on. At the same time, do not implement harsh penalties for those who lose.

Discipline. Some children are quiet and peaceful on the court. They do only what is asked of them. Others are more active. They are eager to try nearly everything, and are always ready for more. Some of these eager ones are nearly out of control.

Children who are out of control do not pay attention, are frequently off task, take more than their share of the parent's time, and lead others astray. They are more likely than their peers to disregard their neighbors, and engage in hazardous activities like running wildly, hitting tennis balls "full blast" in all directions, and swinging rackets like bats or clubs.

They may be well behaved in one-on-one situations but in a group they tax the patience of even the most gentle of souls. In fact, older children like this are probably better at getting in and out of trouble than parents and teachers are in correcting it. These children command a great deal of time and attention from everyone, including parents.

Good planning and good time management reduce discipline problems. Poor planning and poor management foster misbehavior. Children who lack self-control or self-discipline require special attention. Their misbehavior can be reduced with time outs and redirection. This is reviewed by Gregg Presuto in Chapter 3, practical techniques in the psychology of teaching young children. See pages 29-35.

Summary

Children enjoy activity. They enjoy playing. This is important. Strength, speed and agility are qualities that contribute to success in competitive situations, but have little to do with enjoyment in playful situations.

All in all, two deficiencies require great persistence by students and patience by parents to overcome. They are lack of movement experiences during early childhood and poor hand-eye coordination.

Children may monopolize the parent's attention because they are either well skilled or continually in trouble. However, most children under the age of nine are very cooperative. They are very willing to do what is asked of them. They can make noticeable progress toward becoming respectable little tennis players. More often than not, young children are eager to learn and they are always ready to have fun.

CHAPTER 3

SELF-HELP TEACHING SKILLS

The teaching methods used with Munchkins are different from the traditional way sports are taught to older players. It can be summarized as less talk and more action. The need for special teaching methods for young children is dictated by their nature — active. Parents are encouraged to learn these new teaching skills on their own through. This can be done by reading and studying Munchkin Tennis.

Children require activities that are led by parents and teachers. Young children are less able to work on their own, and they learn at a slower pace than their older brothers and sisters. Finally, young children cannot be expected to "work" at becoming skillful players. However, they will "play" at fun-filled tennis activities endlessly.

While older players begin to "play tennis" after the first few group lessons, younger children may play very little "real" tennis nor will they play when their parents are not present. As a result, playful games are a more effective way to teach Munchkins the skills of tennis than the more business-like manner that is common in class situations where repetitive drills dominate.

Children are serious about play. In a 1988 study conducted by the Institute for the Study of Youth Sports, dull practices and the absence of fun were two important reasons children dropped out of sport activities. This confirms previous studies about sport dropouts. Parents should adopt a playful and flexible attitude when planning and conducting activities for their children.

Playfulness is a light, carefree state where children and parents participate in tennis activities on equal terms. For those who have forgotten about play, remember about climbing trees, playing catch, shooting basketballs, or swimming with neighborhood friends. Time went by rapidly but there was no goal to learn new skills, although learning did occur. Then, the intent was to have fun.

Children, and most adults, have fun playing sports when they are active. Time moves rapidly but not when they are standing in line watching or waiting for others.

The physical skills of tennis are learned best by doing them over and over. When dealing with young children, however, this should not take place in repetitive drills. New skills and reminders about proper techniques can be incorporated into the activity or game when appropriate.

Munchkins learn better with the proper guidance from the tennis instructors.

The objective of this section on teaching methods is simple. It is to review techniques for creating as much activity as possible during formal or informal sessions with Munchkins. This may require that serious parents examine their goals or priorities. Quality of performance should take a back seat to other considerations. In other words, maximum participation and fun must occur, not developing well-schooled strokes.

In addition to teaching methods, this chapter includes the psychology of coaching. Special emphasis is placed on learning to establish a more positive sport scene using techniques that make learning more enjoyable.

Take A.I.M. on Time

It has been stated repeatedly that players learn sport skills best by doing them. Doing is: participation, opportunity to try, trials, and time on task. Time is the primary focus here. Group classes and individual practice sessions can be divided into four kinds of time: Activity Time, Instructional Time, Management Time and a most unproductive and troublesome Standing In Line Time.

Suppose you conduct 10 lessons and each one lasts for an hour. You will have 10 hours to make your key teaching points and help players become more skillful. What can you expect to accomplish during these 10 hours? Most beginning students in college physical education classes require eight to 10 hours of group instruction to play a new sport with skill and understanding. Beginners can become self-directed learners in this length of time. Let us examine learning time in more detail.

Keeping Munchkins active at all times is a necessary component of a successful program.

Management Time. Management Time is the time used to get the courts ready for lessons, moving players here and there, getting drinks, taking shade breaks and going to the bathroom. Setting out markers, drawing lines, adjusting nets, getting charts and clipboards, and picking up tennis balls are other examples of management time.

These tasks are indispensable but contribute little or nothing to actual learning. Therefore, it should consume no more than 10% of actual lessons or court time. This equals six minutes in a 60-minute lesson.

Instructional Time. Instructional Time is important in learning, obviously. This is the time devoted to telling, demonstrating, viewing and otherwise imparting tennis skills, game strategies and knowledge to players. Talks about the forehand, backhand, foot position, racket preparation or follow through are also features of instructional time as are evaluative chalk talks.

As with Management Time, it is best to keep Instructional Time short, particularly with Munchkins. Again, Instructional Time should consume no more than 10% of actual lesson or court time. That too consumes just six minutes in a 60-minute lesson.

Some people mistakenly believe that beginners need more instruction than advanced players. Actually, beginners cannot absorb as much as can more-advanced players. Therefore, pick out the key points to emphasize, limit instructional messages to no more than two or three related thoughts, and then get the players into activity time.

Activity Time. Most learning in tennis, as with all sports, occurs during activity time. Active learning time, referred to as academic learning time (ALT) in classroom studies, is the time spent stroking the ball, serving, and otherwise practicing skills with the ball on the court. Activity Time should consume 80% of actual court or practice time. That is 48 minutes in a 60-minute lesson.

As Munchkins stay active during the lesson, they learn more and everybody's time remains productive.

However, there is more to it than that. Activity time should be viewed in relation to how many children are active at one time. Consider it activity time when 51% of the students are active, simultaneously. It requires careful planning to maintain this level of activity. Of course, if you are "playing" only with your child, it is easier to maintain a high level of activity time.

Standing In Line Time. There is one additional unit of time that merits attention. It is standing in line and is commonly seen in weak teaching, basketball lay up drills, or goal shooting in soccer. SILT is neither active learning time nor Instructional Time. It may look like the children are active, but most of them are doing nothing. In fact, a few are waiting for an opportunity to make something happen, to stir up trouble.

Standing in line should be kept to a minimum in play situations. It produces trouble in line time — TILT. It is when those disruptive kids get restless.

When players are arranged in lines, we expect the lines to be straight. We expect the players to be quiet so we can talk, and we expect everyone to pay attention so they can learn from the mistakes of others. Before long, we find ourselves expending more energy controlling the children in line than teaching. Order becomes more important than learning.

Eliminate SILT by using more equipment in less structured activities. Use informal or random formations. For instance, rather than have one player at a time bounce the ball to the net and return, have the players bounce their ball to the net and return, in waves. Instruct as they move and for a brief moment when they return, but keep it brief.

Doing takes time. Management Time and SILT nearly always occur but they contribute little or nothing to learning and performance compared to doing, Activity Time. Instructional Time is important but Activity Time, active learning time, is where skill development occurs. The best learning occurs when a short amount of instructional time is followed by activity time.

When planning, avoid standing in line and elimination games. Make 100% activity the standard by which activities, games and drills are selected. If the activity does not involve 100% participation, look for a different game, change the activity, and replan. We all learn best by doing, and "doing it" is how children learn and have fun at the same time. Plan for 100% activity. (Hutslar, 1985:101-102)

Be Positive

The human relations side of learning can be summarized as "be positive." For parents, teachers and coaches, this involves the use of positive reinforcement, correcting mistakes in a positive way, expecting children to succeed rather than fail, being a good model for them to imitate, proper use of motivation, and an understanding of arousal or excitement. All of this influences how well young children see themselves (i.e., self-concept) and learn tennis skills. This, in turn, determines the relationship that your children will develop with you and tennis in the years ahead.

Do it right and you may develop another tennis partner for life. Do it wrong and they will disappear at the mention of the word

Positive reinforcement should be a cornerstone for any Munchkin Tennis program.

tennis. Do it too well and you may soon have a world class player in the family.

Positive reinforcement. Perhaps the most dramatic change in educational philosophy in the last decade is the way students are motivated to learn. The emphasis has turned from punishment to positive reinforcement.

Positive reinforcement means "be positive." The core of it is feedback. The theory underlying positive reinforcement is that ". . . a reward is linked to some specific act. Youngsters learn they will receive a reward (e.g., positive feedback) when they act in a certain way. Rewards that are commonly used in youth sport are smiles, pats on the back, hand slapping and clapping including high fives, 'ata boys' and 'ata girls,' plus other kind words of praise and encouragement." (Hutslar, 1985:110)

Feedback provides learners with visual or verbal information about the quality of their performance. It is most effective when it immediately follows the trial or event, is corrective rather than derogatory in nature, is specific to a given movement or skill rather than general, and is positive.

Performance improves when children know what they did, what they did not do, and what they are supposed to do. This can be done rather painlessly with what is called a positive sandwich. It is the CCE Principle and was described by Frank L. Smoll and Ronald E. Smith in their 1979 book Improving Relationship Skills in Youth Sport Coaches. C-C-E means compliment, correct, encourage.

Compliment the tennis player on things he or she has been doing well.

Correct a mistake.

Encourage the player by telling him or her that she can do it if she keeps trying.

Expect success. There is more to being positive than smiling and patting children on the back. Educational researchers have discovered that some children fail while having the ability to pass. They fail because they have been treated like failures. Teachers have convinced them they are not capable of doing the work successfully. As a result of this, they quit trying. When they quit trying, they do, in fact, begin to fail.

This downward spiral, known as the self-fulfilling prophecy, is created by treating students like they do not know the answers, cannot do the work, and are incapable of improving. They are treated harshly and given very little attention, positive feedback, time to show what they can do, or time to respond.

For those parents who work with their own children, this research is a clear signal. Children are capable of great accomplishments when they are treated as if they can do it. Treat your children as if they are successful and they will be successful. On the court, it means give each child ample time, attention and trials. Expect them to be successful, and they will be successful.

Modeling. Most of us, but particularly youngsters, learn much from the people with whom we associate. That is, we copy and imitate what we see. Just look at clothing styles, the cars we drive, and the way we talk.

Children copy what they see. Therefore, it is very important that parents and other youth leaders be good models for children.

Swear and they swear. Talk nice and they talk nice.

Walk and they walk. Run and they run.

Sit around and they sit around. Get active and they get active.

Play tennis and they play tennis.

Motivation. Much of what has been presented in this chapter falls in the category of motivation. Most children, unlike older students, are eager to play. It is natural, internal and self-generated. In fact, play is rewarding to children, a naturally occurring reward.

The motivation level of young children was illustrated well by responses from mothers with a program in Cincinnati directed by John Weil, a teaching professional. Mothers reported children who slept with their rackets and would not even remove their T-shirts to be washed. How many adults do you know who are this motivated about anything?

The challenge for parents and other adult leaders is to channel this self-generated enthusiasm into tennis activities and games. It can be done with planning.

Start lessons without a plan and anything might happen, including many discipline problems. Plan a variety of activities with 100% participation and everyone will benefit from the fun-oriented nature of young children.

Some children have an "I can't do it" attitude. If this sounds familiar, parents should keep "You can do it!" messages flowing. Tell them about their successful strokes and the good things they do so they do not get down on their performance. Do not let children feel they are less capable than other players because they do not hit the ball as well as others.

At the same time, do not allow youngsters to make fun of each other or call each other nasty names. All of these little words of encouragement add up to creating a warm, supportive positive atmosphere where youngsters can be themselves, learn tennis and have fun.

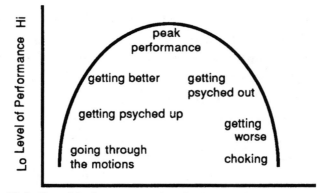

Relationship between stimulation and performance

Arousal. This is an aspect of motivation that most people know as "psyching up" and "psyching out" players. It concerns the child's level of excitement, attention or alertness, and operates in both lessons and match situations.

The illustration above shows it as a relationship between performance level and motivation or stimulation. When motivation increases, performance tends to increases. When motivation becomes too high or intense, performance decreases.

The performance of unskilled players suffers in high arousal situations. Skillful players may perform well in high arousal situations. When stimulation becomes too high, the performance of all players may suffer. It is commonly known as "choking."

However, the response to stimulation, good or bad, varies from person to person. Therefore, parents should know how each player responds to motivation, arousal, or stimulation.

Parents who work with more skillful players should find out who needs motivation, who does not respond well to high arousal, and who should be left alone. When in doubt, find out.

Information about arousal should be prefaced with a reminder about reality. Children are already motivated. Most do not need stimulation. They may, in fact, need to slow down and calm down.

Self concept. Self-concept describes how people feel about themselves and is similar in meaning to self-esteem, self-worth, self-image, self-respect and ego.

Self-concept is learned and, in the case of children, develops based on how they are treated by others. Abusive remarks about level of play, mistakes, misbehavior and personal characteristics tear down self-esteem.

Tell children how "bad" they are and they will begin to see themselves as worthless. Tell them they are good, nice, smart, skilled, well behaved or special and they will see themselves as important human beings, a most valuable person.

Feeling good about yourself is part of enjoying tennis and wanting to return day after day. This helps children learn, improve, and play up to their potential.

Practical techniques in the psychology of teaching young children

Working with children involves continual learning. There is always more to learn. Working with your own child, one on one, may be your first step toward becoming a group instructor, or even a tennis pro.

Parents and tennis teachers should exhibit the following qualities when working with children.

• Be confident. Be knowledgeable so you can explain what you are doing and be able to justify it to others.

• Believe that working with children is important. Parents can establish lifetime activity patterns in children through tennis. These influences can go well beyond tennis.

• Be responsible. Plan lessons carefully. Have all equipment and teaching aids ready.

• Enjoy working with children. Have fun with children.

• Encourage your children. Do not let them adopt an "I can't do that!" attitude. Continually remind them that they can do it if they stay at it. They will be successful if they keep trying.

• Have a sense of humor. Look for opportunities to spice up lessons by reacting to situations on the court. Do funny things. Say funny things. Gregg Presuto will "head" the ball or "take a fall" when hit by a stray ball. Do not make fun of them. Laugh with the children, not at them.

• Help students develop confidence in themselves. Confidence comes from competence. It can come from their ability to play tennis, moving in a physical environment, and getting along with others.

Practical tips. Some practical tips help parents become more effective in group situations.

• Make a good impression the first day. Have a plan and know your objectives. Dress neatly and be on time. Answer questions for children and parents. Explain what will occur and then get started promptly.

• Use your voice effectively. Use simple language with good grammar. Inflections and hand or body gestures help emphasize important points.

• Speak clearly. Face your students and project your voice over the area. Do not chew gum, pencils, fingers, tobacco and sunglasses while teaching.

• Keep directions short. Make two or three points and then get everyone active. Review frequently.

• Use short, positive statements. Identify what students are to do and when they do it correctly. Do not berate them with negative comments or verbal abuse.

• Motivate with words and actions. Identify their errors and their accomplishments in a nice way. Use words and phrases like "Move those magic feet" to help them see what they need to do. Use phrases and terms with which they are familiar.

• Redirect effectively. Find out the source of problems. Sometimes directions are unclear or too complicated. Do not get impatient when children do not follow directions. Repeat the directions or simplify them and try again.

The attention of small children strays easily. Here are some ways to keep them on task.

- Specific praise. Saying "good stroke" over and over is not enough. Children need to know why the ball they just hit was a good shot. Otherwise, they may stop doing the right things. Be specific. For example, you might say: "Billy, that was a great forehand. You hit the ball over the net and into the backcourt."

- Keep it short and simple. The attention span of Munchkins is short. When explaining activities, games, strokes or drills, use short demonstrations with few words. Break complicated movements into simple parts, then put them together in whole activities or games.

- Provide continuous reinforcement. Maintain a good learning atmosphere and good behavior by praising correct responses. Extra turns, prizes and after class drinks can be used to maintain attention and good behavior.

Shy children

Shy children may not participate as fully as other children. Occasionally, a child may not even come on the court. Learning is inhibited when they "need" to be with the parent, sibling or friend. In fact, they may actually hang onto them for comfort. This disrupts others. Here is how parents can help shy children.

- Be patient. Shy children stand out quickly, even when parents or siblings do not tell you. The first rule is to avoid forcing them into situations that upset them even more.

- Be encouraging. Shy children listen. Do not ignore them because they do not play or do what you say. Encourage them in a friendly way to participate with everyone else. Invite them to join in when they are ready.

- Shaping. Let them become comfortable with other players, and reduce their dependency on others. This may take several lessons, perhaps a series of lessons. Keep in mind that, when they return, it is evidence you are on the right track. Try these statements to reduce shyness:

"Sally! You do not have to play if you do not want to. Just come on the court and watch for a while."

"John! If you like, you can help us pick up some tennis balls now."

"Mary! Will you join us in this game and try it for a while."

Disruptive children

Disruptive children create a distinct set of problems for parents, teachers, coaches and classmates. Unlike older brothers and sisters, young children are not usually belligerent, mean to others, or even uncooperative. In fact, most children are quite likable, but disruptive children do test your patience.

In some cases, their behavior may appear to a novice as hyperactivity, called attention deficit syndrome. These children may be unable to control themselves for any length of time. Most likely, parents are aware of this. If not, refer parents to the professional community.

Misbehavior at this young age seems to be linked to over-activity that includes constant talking, fidgeting, poking, stirring up trouble, and leading others astray. They may pay attention to all the wrong things, swing rackets, throw or swing wildly at any tennis ball, or run full speed at every opportunity. What ever level of activity they exhibit, they have difficulty focusing on the tasks at hand.

Parents must remind themselves that these children are not malicious. Untrained leaders and parents might become annoyed at them personally and resort to verbal abuse, even physical punishment. As everyone knows, this produces little long-lasting change.

In dealing with disruptive children, it is important not to attack the will or character of disruptive children. Focus on their behavior.

Personal attacks on the character of children are ineffective, and destroy self-esteem. As we know from experience, these children will be in trouble again soon. It is predictable.

There are four positive ways to change the behavior of disruptive children. They work without attacking the children. They focus on behavior. Techniques include planned ignoring, token economies, punishment, and redirection.

Planned ignoring. Many people say that children misbehave to get the attention of classmates or adults. They are not seeking punishment. They want to be noticed, whether a clown or agitator.

It takes valuable time from the group to stop this behavior, particularly if it is just a minor irritant. When misbehavior is minor, ignore it. If it is more serious, try one of the following techniques.

Token economy. This strategy involves paying children with redeemable coupons or tokens for their accomplishments. When used to correct misbehavior, children might receive a token for every 5, 10, or 15 minutes of good behavior. They can trade tokens for desirable things like drinks, items from the pro shop, free court time, extra coaching time from the teacher, or treats by parents.

On the practical side, someone must pay for these incentives. There is also the chance that others may want tokens. A few crafty children may start misbehaving in order to gain tokens for good behavior. Plan token economies carefully and note all the consequences.

It is desirable to wean players from token economies, eventually. The intention of token economies is that children begin to control or direct their behavior without outside incentives.

Punishment. This is negative reinforcement. When misbehavior continues, it wastes valuable time and may injure others. Sometimes punishment is required but it should not be physically or verbally abusive.

Running, sit ups and push ups are traditional punishments in sport. Yet, they are important conditioning activities. By making children do these to atone for misbehavior, they may learn to hate the very activities that will help them become better players. Do not use conditioning activities as punishment.

Instead, remove the child from the activity for a short period of time. Call it a "time out," a short period of inactivity. Just send them to the side and ask them to return when they can behave. Remember that play is a naturally occurring reward for children. They like to play so making them sit out for a short time can lead to improved behavior.

Redirection. This is a technique where children who misbehave are told what they are doing wrong, what they are supposed to do, and when they are doing it, exhibiting good behavior. It can be done in conjunction with "time outs."

A Discipline Plan. A progressive discipline plan for disruptive children is outlined next. Follow these steps:
1. Ask them to stop what they are doing.
2. Next time, ask them if they know what they are doing. If not, tell them. Then ask them to stop.
3. Next, tell them what they are not to do and what they are supposed to do.
4. The next time it occurs, ask them to take a time out. Ask them to return ready to play and behave.
5. Next, expel them from the activity for the remainder of the day. Ask them to return the next day ready to play and behave.
6. Next, expel them from the next session. Ask them to return the following day ready to play and behave.
7. When misbehavior continues, sit down with the individual and possibly a parent. Develop a written contract that spells out what the child will do during the activity. It is to be signed by all parties.

8. Finally, when children cannot follow the contract, expel them from the activity for good. This should be the last resort. (Adapted from Hutslar, 1985:119)

Gregg Presuto, a tennis pro and Munchkin Tennis innovator, conducts Munchkin Tennis in Chester, New Jersey and at the Van der Meer Tennis Center on Hilton Head Island, South Carolina. He summarized his thoughts on working with small children in this way. "You do not need a Ph.D. in child psychology to work with small children. Just realize that understanding small children starts with patience, and acquiring a lot of practical experience. It is a continual process. You can learn it on your own a bit faster if you read and study manuals such as The USPTR Manual of Munchkin Tennis."

Portions of the material on the psychology of teaching children were provided by Gregg Presuto. He holds a Bachelor's degree in Psychology from Averett College in Virginia, is a USPTR Professional, and is the head pro at Fox Chase Racquet Club in Chester, New Jersey. Presuto teaches Munchkin Tennis at his club, the Van der Meer Tennis Center and conducts USPTR Early Child Development Munchkin Clinics nationally and internationally.

Action formations for activities and games

The formations that parents use for their activities and games determine the activity level and learning opportunities for children. For instance, relay games with teams in single file usually involve one active player running with a ball or racket while all others wait, jump around and cheer. Relay formations produce excitement, energy, noise and performance under pressure of competition. However, learning occurs best in other formations where players have more trials or attempts. The basic formations for sport action include:

• single file used in relay races

X X X X X X

O O O O O O

• shuttle relay with two single files facing one another

X X X X X ——————— X X X X X

• partners in pairs and triples

      X   X   X   X

X X   X   X X   X X   X X

• zig zag formation with four or more players

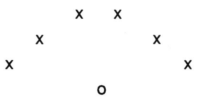

• semi-circle with a central player

          X   X

      X   X

    X   X

        O

• line formations with a central player

X X X X X

O

• lines or waves

X   X   X   X   X

• parallel lines facing each other

X   X   X   X   X

O   O   O   O   O

• circles

```
        X       X
     X               X
  X                     X
  X                     X
     X               X
        X       X
```

• random placement in the activity space

Avoid formations that result in standing in line and games that rely on elimination. Select formations that provide the greatest amount of activity time. Children will learn more, behave better, and have more fun.

Teaching Stations

Teaching stations are similar to coaching stations or circuit training. They involve conducting two or more compatible activities at the same time with one or more leaders. Children rotate systematically from one station to the next, spending a short time at each.

A parent helps students at one station. Students work on previously-learned activities at another station on their own. When assistants or other parents are available, they can monitor the other stations.

When children work at stations on their own, three things help them stay on task. First, post signs or markers at each station that identify the task to be performed. Second, they can repeat activities they know and have done successfully in the past.

Third, specific tasks can be printed on individual cards, task cards. Task cards are like grade cards. They list tennis tasks or skills. Students write down the number of trials completed each day. For instance, tasks might include 20 Ups & Downs, 15 Forehand Wall Rallys, 10 Partner Bumps, or 25 Rope Jumps.

Stations increase Activity Time, reduce Management Time, and increase learning. In addition, standing in line waiting for a turn is eliminated, as are the discipline problems that accompany inactivity. For young children, a three-station program might include:

Station 1: Munchkin Tennis with parent

Station 2: Ups & Downs, 20

Station 3: Rope jumping, 25

Students can spend five minutes at each station. The parent leads Station 1. Children complete the tasks designated at Stations 2 and 3. On signal, children at Station 1 move to Station 2. Children at Station 2 move to Station 3. Children at Station 3 move to Station 1. Rotate again in 5 minutes. In 15 minutes, each child will spend 5 minutes with a parent and 10 minutes in two self-directed activities. The activity might conclude with a game using these skills.

Summary

Teaching children to play tennis, and doing it well, requires special skills by parents, instructors, teachers, and coaches. Just as there are basic skills in tennis, there are basic skills in teaching. They include knowing something about young children compared to older children and adults, planning, teaching methods (Take A.I.M. on Time), teaching the skills of tennis, and being a positive influence.

The focus of this chapter was on becoming an effective teacher and how to be a more positive influence on children. The previous chapter presented characteristics that help parents understand young children. The next several chapters deal with the skills of tennis.

Use the NAYSI Teacher Self-help Checklist on the next two pages to evaluate your teaching skills. Good teachers have a good influence on how well students acquire new skills. Rate yourself periodically. If you score about the same each time, read and study The USPTR Manual of Munchkin Tennis to improve and rate yourself again.

NAYSI Teacher Self-help Checklist

Directions: Teachers rate themselves with this self-help form. Compare yourself to past performance or to others. Circle the number (5 is high, 1 is low) that best describes yourself now. Write your Total Score at the bottom of the page and divide that score by 27 (or actual number of items checked) to obtain the Average Score. There is a positive relationship between effective teaching and student achievement. Eliminate weaknesses and maintain or improve strengths. (Based in part on *Beyond X's and O's* by Jack Hutslar)

Very good, I consider myself quite good at this
1   Good, I am better than most
.   2   Average
.   .   3   Below average, would benefit from self study
.   .   .   4   Among the least able at this time
.   .   .   .   5   Unable to rate myself on this item
.   .   .   .   .   U

My Teaching Skills

1	2	3	4	5	U	1	Management time in class is short
1	2	3	4	5	U	2	Move from one activity to the next without undue delays
1	2	3	4	5	U	3	Instructional time is short — lectures and talks
1	2	3	4	5	U	4	Know the subject matter
1	2	3	4	5	U	5	Read and study all materials prior to class
1	2	3	4	5	U	6	Use teaching aids to illustrate facts, ideas and concepts
1	2	3	4	5	U	7	Start at students' knowledge or ability level and then help them progress
1	2	3	4	5	U	8	Probe to determine what students know and understand
1	2	3	4	5	U	9	Evaluate daily progress with formative questions or instruments
1	2	3	4	5	U	10	Review to correct mistakes when errors are found in daily learning
1	2	3	4	5	U	11	Stay on task myself and keep students on task
1	2	3	4	5	U	12	Read and study to improve

							teaching skills
1	2	3	4	5	U	13	Speak clearly and use good grammar
1	2	3	4	5	U	14	Face students, not wall or board, when speaking
1	2	3	4	5	U	15	Am aware of my distracting or annoying mannerisms — work to stop them
1	2	3	4	5	U	16	Use humor with students where possible and appropriate
1	2	3	4	5	U	17	Set a good example for students to copy
1	2	3	4	5	U	18	High activity time characterizes my instructional methods
1	2	3	4	5	U	19	Doing activities take priority over lectures
1	2	3	4	5	U	20	Learning is the most important objective in my classes
1	2	3	4	5	U	21	All students participate in class - no withdrawing permitted
1	2	3	4	5	U	22	Use positive reinforcement to help students learn
1	2	3	4	5	U	23	Do NOT prejudge students based on the comments of others
1	2	3	4	5	U	24	Expect each student to do well, learn and improve
1	2	3	4	5	U	25	Insist that students treat each other mannerly, with dignity and respect
1	2	3	4	5	U	26	I am a better teacher now than last year. I improved. If not, why?
1	2	3	4	5	U	27	My overall rating of my own teaching skills

_____ Total Score
_____ Average Score (Total divided by 27 or number of items scored)

This rating form may not be altered, transferred or reproduced for commercial distribution without written permission of the author.

Write: Dr. Jack Hutslar, North American Youth Sport Institute, 4985 Oak Garden Drive, Kernersville NC 27284, telephone 919-784-4926.

CHAPTER 4

BASIC SKILLS OF MUNCHKIN TENNIS

The model or theoretical framework upon which Munchkin Tennis is built can be organized around three words. They are people, sport, and a philosophy. More specifically, they are:

This chapter focuses on tennis and the skills of

Children + Tennis = Fun

Munchkin Tennis. It describes the basic skills that young children can learn. In time, it shows what many young children will be able to do after they have "played" with their parents or participated in two or three series of lessons.

Informal play with a parent might occur in five to 30 minutes periods over a number of years. Formal lessons may cover several years and include six to 10 lessons over two to five weeks. Whatever the circumstances, exposure to the skills of Munchkin Tennis will prepare your children for regulation, full court tennis by the age of nine or 10.

Tennis activities for children should be a steady diet of excitement and fun. When this occurs, your children will be eager to play. Then, the transition from Munchkin Tennis to full court tennis will occur as a natural step in their learning progression. Yet, many Munchkin Tennis games provide great practice activities, even for adult players.

Leadership. Adult leadership is more important with nine and under age groups, than older age groups. This is necessary because young children are very dependent on others, even older brothers and sisters, for what they do. As a result, the attitudes, motivations and behavior of parents and tennis instructors is crucial to the success of young children in tennis.

Skills for parents to learn. Parents can learn skills that help children do well. They include:
- Separate children in to one and two year age groups, when working with groups of six or more.
- Set up separate classes for more advanced Munchkins, when possible.
- See that rackets are suitable size and weight.
- Feed balls to Munchkins in a way they will make contact with the ball repeatedly. In other words, hit their racket.
- Adapt or change games, drills, rules and feeds so that each child experiences immediate success. Make tennis fit the children rather than the children fit tennis.
- Use positive motivation and provide a steady flow of encour aging remarks.
- Be specific and tell the children what they are doing correctly even when they do not contact the ball at the correct place in the stroke, "foul off" the ball, or miss it completely.
- Be generous with second chances to hit or try new move ments, even in game situations and matches.
- Be satisfied with a little progress. Even the most awkward children will surprise you with what they are able to accomplish.
- Let them become familiar with new situations slowly, rather than under threat from helpers who may not remember what it is like to be fearful.
- Use good language and halt the negative language of others.
- Treat everyone fairly, without biases and in a friendly manner.
- Help them hit the ball, keep the ball in play between the lines and have fun.

Skills for players to learn. There are many coaching points to learn so young children can hit tennis balls well. The actual skills can be identified rather precisely.

Munchkin Tennis allows children to learn a variety of skills that can help them in other sports as well.

Yet, no matter how hard parents work, most young children will not absorb everything there is to know. In fact, the most predictable feature of this age group is that if you "work" at tennis in drill-like situations, you may drive them away. They will not return to play again.

When parents "play" at activities and games using these skills, Munchkins will return again and again. Why? Because it is fun.

A common approach to skill development with young children was described by John Weil, tennis pro at the Racket Club at Harpers Point in Cincinnati, Ohio. He said:

"In my children's program, I have tried to avoid making a list of skills but I have them in the back of my mind. My goal is to sneak them in."

Tennis skills that most instructors teach in their programs include the grip, forehand, backhand, a short volley-type stroke used near the net, a bounce and overhand serve, and overhead. Other skills and teaching points receive varying amounts of attention. It depends on the skill level of the children and their ability to put it into practice. They are: grip, firm wrist, watching the ball, straight-racket arm(s), one-hand forehand bump, one-hand forehand groundstroke, one- or two-hand backhand bump, one- or two-hand backhand groundstroke, forehand bump and volley at the net, backhand bump and volley at the net, side to the net to hit bumps and groundstrokes, ready position with racket pointed toward the net or instructor, racket back in preparation for groundstrokes, moving the feet (magic feet) while turning side to the net, weight shift from front foot to back foot, contact point in front of the hip, racket parallel to court, racket face perpendicular to the ground, follow-through on groundstrokes toward the net post, moving to hit the ball, shifting feet to hit alternate forehands and backhands, maintaining proper distance from the ball, bounce serve and self feed to start a rally, overhead, serving, and court position.

The grip on the racket may be a source of disagreement. In speaking with many instructors, no single grip was preferred. Few were even concerned with it. Some instructors may teach the grip a certain way. Others say, let the kids grip it however they pick up the racket.

Major teaching points that help all players hit the ball consistently are: watch the ball, turn side to the net, move the feet to help judge the distance from the ball, racket take-back, racket face perpendicular to the court, and follow through. Many unsuccessful hits can be traced back to these points.

In addition to these more obvious skills, young children also learn hand-eye coordination, ball-racket relationships, ball sense, reacting to bouncing balls, and force. They improve their ability to move to the ball, move when the ball is hit directly at them, stopping and starting on the court, and court coverage. They also learn counting, where to start, scoring, getting along with others, taking turns and sharing. The Munchkin Skills Checklist is presented on the last page of this chapter. Reproduce it, as needed, for discussion and evaluation purposes with children and parents.

Safety. Risk management is an overriding concern in sport today. While tennis is very safe compared to many other activities, young children still need many reminders about safety.

For instance, beginners need to learn that tennis rackets are not  swords, axes, baseball bats or hockey sticks, unless used as such in the supervised activities and games noted in later chapters. Teach safe racket skills.

Ask them to keep the racket head below waist level. Remind them that the racket is used to hit tennis balls only, not heads and hands, nets and fences.

Some children thoughtlessly hit or kick any stray tennis ball. Again, they must be told what you want them to do with stray balls rather than knock them about aimlessly.

Some children are very active and run with little self-control. They can crash into other children, trip on nets and fences or injure themselves by slipping on balls or damp courts.

Bandaids should be kept handy to prevent "hot spots" from becoming sore and swollen blisters. Proper shoes and clothing for the weather can make tennis enjoyable.

Regular water and shade breaks are mandatory on hot and humid days. Breaks at 15-minute intervals are common. **Never, but never, should water be withheld from children (or any other person) in order to motivate them to try harder or behave. Let youngsters drink all the water they want.**

Prudent parents should instruct children in proper skills, warn them of hazardous activities, always be present when youngsters are in their care, and insure. (Hutslar, 1985:154-155.) Keep safety a prominent aspect of Munchkin Tennis. See that preventable accidents do not detract from their ability to have fun.

Competence builds self-esteem. Parents will be pleased to learn that children who engage in physical activity programs like tennis become more out-going or overt, expressive and self-confident. Learning to move successfully in the physical world develops

self-esteem.

The success of young children is increased when parents: (1) praise students for the skills when they try hard and do well, (2) provide corrective feedback about the skills needed to hit balls and play games, and (3) "put" their tosses and feeds where youngsters swing. In other words, hit their rackets.

The time that young children spend on the court is not wasted. They learn and they improve, particularly when it is fun.

Munchkins are happiest when they're having fun and learning something. Their self-esteem inevitably improves.

In fact, when Munchkins are compared to new players of the same age, Munchkins perform better. They even surpass some older children. Munchkins have better hand-eye coordination, ball sense, and ball-racket relationships. They are comfortable with bouncing balls, grips, strokes, force, and scoring. They know how to move to the ball, move when the ball is hit directly at them, stop and start on the court, and court positioning. While all of this may occur, Munchkin Tennis can be condensed to a few central ideas. They are:

- keep the ball on the court between the lines,
- play a variety of tennis games, and
- have fun doing it.

Etiquette in tennis. Etiquette is the manners of tennis. There are some points about sportsmanship and etiquette that should be a part of the learning process, even at this young age. They include:

- Keep play moving briskly so others are not kept waiting.
- Do not wave rackets or throw balls to distract others.
- What do you do with stray balls that come onto your court?
- How do you retrieve your ball when it goes in another court?
- What is proper talk on the courts. Today, it is common to hear young children make loud, boisterous, rude and nasty comments.

Good behavior and proper etiquette make tennis an enjoyable experience for everyone.

- How do you treat and talk with other children. Generally speaking, leaders should not allow children to ridicule and make uncomplimentary remarks to others.
- Talk nice and be nice to each other.
- Play it over when there are disagreements.
- Accept victory graciously and defeat without bitterness or excuses.
- Keep score honestly.
- Try hard, play fair and have fun.

Good behavior and proper etiquette are expected from all children, regardless of age. It should occur on or off the tennis courts. In return, youngsters should receive good instruction plus fair and just treatment from their leaders. The following section specifies what children can be expected to learn as well as their rights they should expect to receive.

Objectives. Objectives provide specific information about what is to be taught and learned. The skills that young children acquire during tennis fall into several categories or domains. Traditionally, in physical education, they are referred to as cognitive (knowledge), affective (attitudes), and motor (skills).

What children learn in formal lessons can be carefully planned. Informally, they also pick up or "catch" other skills, mannerisms, ways of talking, and how to treat others. This is done through their association with parents, other adults and their peers. Parents must be aware of what children learn informally. What they "catch" can be more influential than what they learn in formal lessons.

Objectives of Munchkin Tennis include the social skills needed to work in group situations, individual tennis skills, game skills and the physiological changes that occur as a result of vigorous physical activity. The following list of objectives provides guidance in selecting activities for young children.

Objectives of activities and games in Munchkin Tennis

Social Objectives
1. Have fun
2. Listen, pay attention
3. Share
4. Cooperate
5. Treat others well
6. Memory and remembering
7. Be mannerly
8. Play by the rules
9. Sportsmanship and etiquette
10. Teamwork
11. Learn home practice activities
12. Provide lifetime activity and interest in tennis
13. Stimulate mental functioning
14. Develop self-confidence
15. Improve self-esteem

Individual Tennis Skill Objectives
16. Watch the ball
17. Develop hand-eye coordination
18. Judge proper distance from ball
19. Develop racket and ball control
20. Learn grip and stance
21. Self-feed to start play
22. Track ball in flight
23. Move to the ball
24. Develop footwork
25. Move feet to get side to net
26. Bend knees to retrieve low balls or shots
27. Evasive action to move away from ball
28. Hit the ball in a specific direction
29. Hit a specific target or area

30. Hit ball with control, not power
31. Hit the ball over the net with control
32. Consistency
33. Adjust for spin on the ball
34. Balance
35. Fast reaction to the ball, reflex action
36. Move quickly with racket control
37. Hit ball on bounce, in air
38. Use strokes with accuracy
39. Develop soft net shot with control

Game Objectives
40. Learn parts of court
41. Count and keep score
42. Learn tennis scoring system
43. Combine movement and strokes
44. Run, stop and volley
45. Court position and coverage
46. Use backhand or serve in game situation
47. Use skills in game situation
48. Learn to play tennis

Physiological Objectives
49. Develop wrist and arm strength
50. Improve leg strength and power
51. Improve conditioning
52. Use speed, agility and rapid change of direction
53. Improve speed and endurance
54. Run fast, stop quickly and change direction
55. Drink plenty of water on hot and humid days
56. Improve tolerance for physical activity
57. Feel good from vigorous play
58. Have fun in vigorous play

The Bill of Rights for Young Athletes is another way to look at what young children should expect from sport experiences. It was drafted in 1977 by the Youth Sports Task Force of the American Alliance for Health, Physical Education, Recreation and Dance as is reprinted on page 54 with permission of the Alliance.

Summary

The skills and objectives noted in this chapter provide ample "curriculum" material, whether taught or caught. Some Munchkins will learn more than others. Most young children will not learn it all, nor will older children. The point in presenting these skills and objectives is to remind parents that they are a part of many fun-filled activities and games.

The Bill of Rights for Young Athletes

1. Right of the opportunity to participate in sports regardless of ability level.
2. Right to participate at a level that is commensurate with each child's developmental level.
3. Right to have qualified adult leadership.
4. Right to participate in safe and healthy environments.
5. Right of each child to share in the leadership and decision-making of their sport participation.
6. Right to play as a child and not as an adult.
7. Right to proper preparation for participation in the sport.
8. Right to an equal opportunity to strive for success.
9. Right to be treated with dignity by all involved.
10. Right to have fun through sport.

Munchkin Skills Checklist

Name _____ Age _____

Telephone _____ Class Time _____

Munchkin progress report for discussion with children and parents.

Key: + very good   √ satisfactory   – not ready yet

____ grip
____ ready position
____ watches the ball
____ racket preparation with side to net
____ contacts ball early
____ follow through
____ forehand
____ backhand
____ forehand volley
____ backhand volley
____ can throw ball into service court
____ can do a bounce serve from self-feed
____ overhead serve & overhead
____ ball and racket control
____ hand-eye coordination, makes ball contact
____ footwork, moves right and left to play balls
____ keeps ball inside the white lines
____ can hit easy and hit hard
____ plays games with partners & opponents
____ can name areas of the court
____ scorekeeping, counting, rules
____ listens, behaves and shows self-control
____ has fun
____ overall performance

Comments:

CHAPTER 5

MUNCHKIN I, MOVEMENT EDUCATION, JUGGLING AND TENNIS TASKS

This chapter, for young beginners, is the first of four-consecutive chapters that describe tennis activities and games for children. The purpose of these activities is to introduce the basic skills of tennis to beginners, ages 4 to 9, in an enjoyable way. They are fun and foster lifelong interest and participation in tennis.

Munchkin I begins with a description of the movement education approach to tennis. Then, a short section on juggling follows. It concludes with a variety of racket and ball skills in a progression. These skills will prepare children for more advanced tennis games in the chapters that follow.

Munchkin II presents many low-organized games. Munchkin III follows with lead-up games. Munchkin IV covers the Graduated Tennis Method (GTM) of instruction in this developmental progression or sequence.

Start with movement education

Some children may have their first play experience with balls when they enroll in Munchkin Tennis. When this is the case, children will become more at ease with ball and racket when they begin each session with simple ball-handling activities. In fact, it can be repeated from session to session and season to season.

There is a well-accepted way to do this for children age nine and under. It is through a method of teaching physical education called movement education.

Movement education, known also as movement exploration, is a style or method of teaching that relies on open-ended questions and statements rather than precise demonstrations and repetitive drills. Students are asked to respond to statements and solve problems through physical activity. In doing this, they become mentally involved in the activity. As a result, they tend to remember what they did longer and gain more from their movement experiences than might occur in "follow the leader" type drills. When "movement" is used with tennis questions and statements, children are provided with exciting and enjoyable ways to explore how different types of game balls react. They can manipulate tennis balls, see what light and heavy force does, and respond to ball and racket challenges.

In contrast to traditional methods of teaching and coaching, there are usually no right and wrong responses in movement education. There are only different responses. This is due, in part, to the lack of experience young children have in physical activity. Correctness of response is not at issue here. Teachers proceed care-

Instructors should allow their students to explore and experience how balls can be carried, tossed, hit, stacked, etc.

fully in an effort to maintain the enthusiasm and spontaneous movement of children. This is done without dampening their natural enthusiasm by providing continual feedback about the right and wrong way to do one skill or another.

Teachers simply allow children to explore and experience the way balls can be carried, tossed, caught, bounced, rolled, bumped, hit, chased and stacked. This can be done alone or with partners. This can be done with any ball. This can be done by exchanging balls with other children frequently. This can be done with one, two or three balls. This can be done at home or on the courts.

New ball handlers may have difficulty tossing and catching small fast moving tennis balls. In fact, the rule of thumb regarding ball size for children is:

The smaller the child, the larger the ball should be.

To help these new players, collect an assortment of game balls: basketballs, volleyballs, footballs, soccer balls, beachballs, whiffle balls, fleece balls, and sponge balls. Acquire all kinds of balls, but avoid hard balls used in baseball, field hockey, golf, lacrosse and softball.

Collect an assortment of rackets: tennis rackets, wooden paddles, plastic paddles, table tennis paddles, racquetball rackets, badminton rackets, squash rackets, homemade wood and coat hanger rackets. Acquire all kinds of rackets. Collect bats too. Collect tennis ball cans, towels, markers, hula hoops and other items that can be used as targets, markers and obstacles.

Fundamental Movements

There are eight fundamental locomotor movements used in movement education. They are:

Walk, run, skip, gallop, slide (shuffle), jump, (two foot take off and landing), hop (one foot, same foot), and leap (take off on one foot, land on the other.) Dodging or change of direction is also used. Incorporate these locomotor movements into ball and racket activities.

Running is an important part of tennis for young children. Unlike older children and teenagers, young children enjoy running, particularly when it is done sensibly and in fun. They even like to run around the court to start and finish lessons.

Colleen Cosgrove, a USPTR teaching professional from Princeton, New Jersey said: "Our Pee Wees just love to run and be active. Most older kids would feel like we are working on conditioning if we did the running games with them that we do with the Pee Wees. In fact, Pee Wees would rather run around 10 times than once."

The methods of instruction for movement education are: (1) short statements or challenges, and (2) carefully selected positive statements by parents in response to what children do and say on the courts during activity. Both occur to enrich and improve their ball handling skills.

The following pages describe how to get started. It begins with a typical first lesson.

Initial lessons (i.e., experiences)

A lesson might start on the court with a bag of different balls and a hopper full of tennis balls. The lesson can begin by opening the bag, pouring them onto the court, and asking each child to get a ball. Ideally, you should have a ball for each child. Let them play with them for a short time. Watch what they do.

Now get their attention. Ask them to stop talking, moving and bouncing balls when your hand is raised. Wait until they comply.

Ask them to "find their space" by spreading over the court in a random manner. Move away from others so they do not touch. In random formations, youngsters can bounce and move freely, but under control so they do not collide with others. Remind them to be careful not to kick, hit or throw anything toward someone unless a part of the activity.

Next, tell the children you are going to make some statements and they are to answer by "doing it" with their ball. The following statements illustrate what parents can say to begin movement education activities. Add others as you become more at ease and creative in this unstructured learning strategy.

How to find your space

Suggested activities:
- Find your space on the court with your ball.
- How big (or wide) is your space?
- Show it by spreading your arms.
- Move your space so you do not touch anyone.
- Walk away from your space without the ball, and return. Do not bump into anyone.
- Move away from your space with the ball. Now return.
- Run from your space and return.

One player - One ball
First with a variety of balls, then tennis balls
- Toss ball in the air.
- Toss ball in the air, let it bounce and catch it.
- Toss ball in the air and catch it.
- Toss ball as high as you can.
- Toss ball back over your head and catch it.
- Toss ball in the air, turn around and catch it.
- Turn all the way around and catch it.
- Catch it before it bounces, with one hand.
- Toss ball from hand to hand.

Bouncing the ball
- Bounce the ball.
- Bounce and catch the ball.
- Bounce the ball with two hands.
- Bounce the ball with two hands, fast. Slowly.
- Bounce the ball with one hand.
- Bounce the ball with your foot.

- Can you dribble the ball like a basketball player?
- Can you dribble the ball like a soccer player?
- Can you kick the ball like a football player? (Be careful not to hit anyone with the ball.)
- Can you juggle the ball like a soccer player? Once? Twice? Three times?

Learning about force

- Toss the ball . . . and catch it.
- Toss the ball as high as you can.
- Bounce the ball as hard as you can.
- Toss the ball softly.
- Bounce the ball gently. Quietly.
- Can you catch the ball quietly, without a sound?
- Bounce the ball like a giant.
- Bounce the ball like Tinker Bell. A Smurf.
- How would an octopus play with your ball?
- How would a tennis player use your ball?
- Can you use the ball like an elephant?
- Can you balance on the ball on your stomach?
- Be your favorite animal with the ball.

Moving

- Toss ball forward, catch it yourself.
- Toss ball forward, catch it on first bounce.
- Toss ball forward, catch it on second bounce.
- Toss ball backward, catch it yourself.
- Toss the ball, wait until it stops, and go get it.
- Look where you are. Toss the ball, wait until it stops, go get it, and run back to where you started. (Do not hit or bump into anyone.)

About the tennis court with
and without balls or tennis balls

- Walk around the whole tennis court.
- Skip around the singles court.
- Bounce the ball on the baseline.
- Sit on the service line.
- Bounce ball in the backcourt.
- Roll ball in alley.
- Toss ball over the net and get it.
- Toss ball over net in service court.
- Toss ball in air behind baseline.
- Throw ball over net from baseline.
- Throw ball over net into the backcourt.

Two players — One ball

- Roll ball to your partner.
- Roll ball to partner between legs.
- Do it another way.
- Toss ball to your partner.
- Toss ball to partner over a line, alley, service court, backcourt.
- Toss ball to partner over the net.
- Catch the ball on two bounces.
- Catch the ball on one bounce.
- Catch the ball before it hits the court.

Juggling

Juggling is a skill that develops hand-eye coordination so important in serving and self-feeds. Learning to juggle one, two and then three balls provides young children with yet more practice at ball skills. They can even practice juggling at home.

Juggling begins with one ball and one hand, then two hands. Then a second ball is added using one and then two hands. Finally a third ball is introduced. Repeat each skill 10 to 20 times to develop a consistent toss and relaxed catch.

The toss is made in a circular outside-in motion in a plane just in front of the body. Catch the ball by cradling it in the fingers with the fingers and thumbs gently curled.

Once two or more balls are used, the second ball is tossed when the first ball begins to drop from the top of the arc. For more ideas about juggling see Juggling for the Complete Klutz (1988) by Cassidy and Rimbeaux.

Learn to juggle one tennis ball

- Hold one ball in dominant hand, toss it straight up and catch (cradle) it in same hand.
- Repeat 10-20 times to develop consistent toss to same spot each time.
- Repeat with the other hand.
- Hold one ball in dominant hand, toss it to other hand in gentle arc, then back.
- Repeat 10-20 times to develop consistent toss in same arc each time.

Two balls

- Hold one ball in each hand.
- Toss one ball up, catch it in same hand as toss. Hold other ball.
- Toss other ball, catch it in same hand as toss.
- Repeat 10-20 times to develop consistent toss in same spot each time.
- Alternate one hand and then the other, catching ball in same

hand from which it was tossed.
- Toss both up at the same time.

Learn to juggle two tennis balls

Young children will begin to drop many more balls when moving to this stage. Remind them to watch the ball and provide lots of encouragement.

- Toss one ball up and catch in the other hand.
- Whoops, forgot to switch ball to other hand.
- Toss one ball and then the other, catch in opposite hands. Start with dominant hand.
- Repeat 10-26 times to develop consistent toss.

Learn to juggle two tennis balls — a variation

- Hold both balls in dominant hand.
- Toss one up, then the other, one at a time, using only the dominant hand.
- Keep them going 2, 3, 4 times with one hand.

As shown in the previous two sections, children can learn to improve many ball or hand-eye skills without rackets. It is done through movement education and juggling. In addition to the statements provided, other "challenges" can be developed around ball, racket skills, and locomotor activities.

Parents are encouraged to be imaginative and creative. Movement exploration can be used to expose children to the ball, racket and court skills needed in tennis, to have fun, and to start their lifetime interest and enjoyment in tennis.

Tennis Tasks

The remainder of this chapter outlines a variety of tennis skills that can be presented in a more direct way. That is, children can be asked to do many of these tasks as self-testing "stunts," or challenges. They can be done with "Simon Says" type commands. Unlike movement education, there is less room for them to deviate from the suggested action. However, like movement education, the element of winning, losing, and who is best is absent or greatly reduced.

In most of these activities, children do not compete against one another to see who is better. Yet, some children seem to do this rather instinctively.

Competitive games are introduced in the last few activities. Many games in Chapters 6 and 7 use the Tennis Tasks presented on the following pages. Incorporate these games into daily lessons for excitement and fun.

Many of these activities can be done with children spaced randomly around any tennis court or other unobstructed area. Provide children with self-testing statements or challenges that describe a tennis task or skill.

Parents may elect to start new tennis players on Tennis Tasks rather than movement education. This is fine.

Tennis Tasks presented in this section are grouped in a logical progression for ease of learning, efficient movement of children and use of time, equipment and facilities.

Group One Tasks

1. Grip the racket in one hand
2. Grip the racket in other hand
3. Grip the racket in both hands

Group Two Tasks

4. Hold a ball on racket
5. Hold ball on racket and move around area
6. Roll the ball with racket
7. Roll the ball around obstacles with racket
8. Roll the ball to a partner with racket
9. Pass the ball from one racket to another
10. Drop ball from racket and catch it on bounce

Group Three Tasks

11. Bounce ball downward with racket
12. Bounce ball upward with racket
13. Bounce ball upward, use alternate faces of racket

Group Four Tasks

14. Bounce ball downward with racket while moving
15. Bounce ball upward with racket while moving
16. Bounce ball upward, use alternate faces of racket while moving

Group Five Tasks

17. Toss ball to partner who bumps it back
18. Bump ball back and forth with partner
19. Bump ball back and forth across line with partner
20. Bump ball back and forth across alley with partner
21. Bump ball back and forth over net with partner

Group Six Tasks

22. Hit the ball to a target or target area
23. Drop ball (self-feed) and hit ball to a target

Group Seven Tasks

24. Bounce the ball off any wall
25. Bounce the ball off any wall with partner
26. Bounce the ball off any wall with partner using one racket

Group Eight Tasks

27. Pick up ball from ground with racket
28. Pick up ball from ground with foot and racket

Group Nine Tasks

29. Toss and catch ball over net or obstacle so opponent cannot catch or return it
30. Hit ball over net or obstacle so opponent cannot return it

The tasks

The following tasks introduce children to holding a racket; manipulating a ball with a racket; working with a partner; the court, hitting a target; moving to hit a ball, bumping or blocking a ball with the racket; and hitting a ball with a partner. Finally, children are introduced to some competitive activities where the objective is to hit the ball so an opponent cannot return it successfully. Refer to Chapter 4, Basic Skills of Munchkin Tennis, page 43, for a more-detailed presentation of skills.

For the following tasks, move at a pace that suits most of the children. There is no hurry. Let the children "play" and enjoy them.

Depending on time and skill level of the children, each group of tasks might occupy all or part of a lesson. Youngsters who learn rapidly may complete all tasks in a few lessons. They are arranged in a progression. Keep it simple and make it fun.

Group One Tasks

1. **Grip the racket in one hand**
2. **Grip the racket in other hand**
3. **Grip the racket in both hands**

Suggested activities

- Carry the racket from one place to another.
- Hold the racket with one hand, both hands, right hand, left hand.
- Pass the racket from one hand to another, around your body, around both legs, one leg.
- Pass the racket (line or circle) from one person to another.
- Grip the racket in different ways while learning to identify the: handle, head and throat, frame and strings.
- Use racket to act out other things like guitar, violin, baseball bat, golf club, ax, gun, tray, drum major's baton or mirror.
- How would a witch use a tennis racket?

Group Two Tasks

4. Hold ball on racket

Suggested activities

- Balance ball on racket using one hand.
- With two hands, palm up and palm down, while moving around the court changing directions, slowly, quickly.
- Change body positions with the ball on racket, stand, kneel, sit.

- Change racket position with ball on it, away from body, close to the body, overhead, in front, to side of the body.
- Roll ball around the racket.
- Repeat with 2 balls.
- Describe what happens to your arms, hands, fingers.

5. Hold ball on racket and move around area

- Carry ball on racket while moving using both hands, one hand, palm up, palm down.
- Grip racket by throat, head, handle while moving.
- Carry ball on racket while moving forward, backward, side ways.
- Carry ball on racket while moving around obstacles, court lines or course.

6. Roll the ball with racket

- Push the ball forward with the racket.
- Repeat this while holding the handle with one hand, both hands, right hand, left hand.
- Go forward, backward, sideways to the right, sideways to the left.
- Roll a ball with palm forward, palm toward self or thumb up and thumb down, or forehand side and backhand side of racket.

7. Roll the ball around obstacles with racket

- Roll a ball with racket along a line on the court or floor, on top of a bench
- Zig zag around objects or people
- Push the ball into a goal.
- Move a ball with racket back and forth along a line using one and two hands.

8. Roll the ball to a partner with racket

- Push ball back and forth with a partner.
- Use both faces of racket.
- Move away from partner one step per push.

9. Pass the ball from one racket to another

- Pretend you are pouring hot soup from one bowl to another. The ball is the soup.
- Pass ball from one racket to another without dropping the ball.
- Pass ball from one partner to another.
- Pass racket with ball on it from one person to the next.
- Pass ball to partner standing side by side, face to face, back to back.

10. Drop ball from racket and catch it on bounce

- Drop ball from racket, catch it on racket.
- Drop ball from racket, catch it on racket as children move about the area.
- Drop ball on a target, catch on racket.
- Face partner, drop ball, partner catches it.
- Repeat standing side by side.
- Drop ball on designated target (hula hoop) for partner to catch.
- Partners move from one hula hoop to another making five (5) drop-catches at each station.

Group Three Tasks

11. Bounce ball downward with racket

Suggested activities

- Drop ball and catch it with two hands, one hand, palm up, palm down.
- Toss ball in air and catch it with two hands, one hand, palm up, palm down.
- Drop ball and catch it on racket.
- Drop and bounce ball on racket.
- Bounce the ball high, waist level, low.
- Repeat using palm up, palm down.
- Bounce the ball gently: in front, at side, other side, while turning around.

12. Bounce ball upward with racket

- Toss ball upward and catch it on racket.
- Catch the ball high, waist level, low.
- Repeat using palm up, palm down.
- Toss ball upward and bounce it on racket.
- Palm up, drop ball with racket, hit gently upward.
- Palm down, drop ball with racket, hit it gently upward.
- Place ball on racket and bounce ball upward.
- Toss ball into the air and bounce it off racket.
- Hit and catch ball after each upward bounce.
- Hit the ball upward lightly, with greater force.
- Hit ball upward, let it bounce on court, catch it.
- Hit ball upward and catch it on racket. Then,
- Bounce ball in air on racket 1, 2, 3, 4 . . . times in a row with one hand, both hands, palm up, palm down.
- Repeat with racket in front, at side, while on knees, standing on one foot.
- Vary the height of the bounces.

13. Bounce ball upward, use alternate faces of racket

- Bounce ball using alternate sides of racket.
- Bounce ball on racket and then court with: one hand, other hand, two hands.
- Repeat and grip racket palm down, palm up.
- Repeat while walking about area, on lines of court.

Group Four Tasks

14. Bounce ball downward with racket while moving
15. Bounce ball upward with racket while moving

Suggested activities

- Repeat tasks described in 11, 12 and 13 and add locomotor movements to increase difficulty. Then,
- Bounce ball gently while moving: forward, to the right, to the left.
- Dribble ball forward with the racket.
- Repeat, grip racket with one hand, both hands, right hand, left hand.
- Go forward, backward, sideways to the right, sideways to the left.
- Dribble ball along a line on the court or floor, on top of a bench, zig zag around objects, and into a goal.

16. Bounce ball upward, use alternate faces of racket while moving

- Repeat activities in number 14.
- Bounce ball in the air on racket 1, 2, 3, 4 . . . times in a row while moving forward, backward, to each side using sliding steps.

Group Five Tasks

17. Toss ball to partner who bumps it back

Suggested activities

- Block or bump ball back to partner who tosses ball gently on one bounce.
- With forehand side or palm forward side.
- With backhand side or palm in, side of racket.
- Block high bouncing ball.
- Block low bouncing ball.
- Block balls that do not bounce, forehand and backhand.

18. Bump ball back and forth with partner

- Partners toss ball back and forth at varying heights over the head of players as they reach up with racket and block the ball.
- Partners toss ball high, right and left and block balls coming from different directions. Then,
- Toss ball, hit it forward to partner.
- Toss ball, let it bounce, hit forward to partner.
- Toss ball, hit it forward to target.
- Toss ball, let it bounce, hit forward to target. Then,
- Bounce ball on racket, hit it upward to partner.
- Bounce ball on racket several times and hit it upward to partner.
- Repeat, hold racket palm down, palm up.

19. Bump ball back and forth across line with partner

- Bounce ball back and forth, try to hit line each time.
- Start with underhand, then overhand tosses.
- Use high bounces and low bounces.
- Move closer together, apart.

20. Bump ball back and forth across alley with partner
21. Bump ball back and forth over net with partner

- Hit ball over towel, racket, bench, or net.
- Hit balls using homemade paddles.
- Hit ball to partner, keep it in the alley.
  (Players with difficulty hitting smaller tennis balls can use larger game balls.)

Group Six Tasks

22. Hit the ball to a target or target area

Suggested activities

- Hit ball between two vertical lines, over lines at varying heights, at circular or cartoon targets at varying heights on net, fence, curtain or wall.
- Repeat, move away from wall.
- Stand forehand side to wall and hit ball 2, 3, 4 . . . times in succession.
- Repeat with backhand side to wall.
- Player 1 without racket bounces ball to player 2 with racket who taps ball upward to player 3 who catches it.
- Repeat, grip racket with one hand, two hands.
- Hit ball with right side, left side to tosser.
- Hit high toss, low toss, before it bounces.

23. Drop ball (self-feed) and hit ball to a target

- Drop ball (self-feed) and hit target, with forehand, backhand.
- Drop ball and hit into service court.
- Drop ball and hit into backcourt.
- Drop ball and hit to partner who catches ball on bounce in target area.
- Repeat, toss ball overhead.

Group Seven Tasks

24. Bounce the ball off any wall

Suggested activities

- Bounce ball off wall 5, 10, 15, 20 times in a row.
- Repeat with two bounces, one bounce, no bounces (volley).
- With one hand, two hands, palm forward (forehand), palm back (backhand).
- Hit on, above, or below the space, target area or cartoon target.

25. Bounce the ball off any wall with partner
26. Bounce the ball off any wall with partner using one racket

- Partner tosses ball against wall, player with racket hits on one bounce to player who tossed it.
- Hit ball against wall between vertical lines 4'6", 13'6", 27' or 36' feet apart.
- Toss ball overhead, hit between vertical lines.
- Repeat using the other face of the racket.
- Repeat using one racket.

Group Eight Tasks

27. Pick up ball from ground with racket

Suggested activities

- Draw racket over top of ball resting on surface so ball will roll onto racket.
- Tap resting ball smartly two or three times with racket so it bounces up. Catch it.
- Repeat this across net for taller children who can reach over a net.

28. Pick up ball from ground with foot and racket

- Position ball between outside of foot and racket. Lift foot and ball, drop ball, bounce and catch it.

Group Nine Tasks

29. Toss and catch ball over net or obstacle so opponent cannot catch or return it.

KIDBIT

Nets can be any obstacle. From low to high, they include: court line, rope, towel, bricks, markers, rackets on end, bench, chair, net, fence, seated players, players with rackets, players with brooms, and elevated ropes or poles.

Suggested activities

- Players, in turn, bounce ball to player in middle of semi-circle with racket who bumps it to next player.
- Repeat, with two bounces, one bounce, no bounces (volley), and overhead.
- With one hand, two hands, palm forward (forehand), palm back (backhand).
- Players, in turn, toss ball over obstacle to player in middle of semi-circle with racket bumps it to next player. Then,
- Players throw back and forth to each other over line, towel, rackets, bench, chair, and net.
- In alley, service courts, backcourts.
- Play catch with ball, 1 or 2 bounces.
- Score a point when opponent fails to make a catch, play to 4 points.

30. Hit ball over net or obstacle so opponent cannot return it

- Drop ball off self-feed and hit ball to partner who catches it in a specific area of court.
- From near net, service line, alley, middle of backcourt, baseline.
- With one hand, two hands, palm forward (forehand), palm back (backhand).
- With easy overhead toss and hit.
- Players hit ball back and forth to each other off wall, over line, towel, bench, chair, and net.
- Players hit ball with racket, paddles or balloon rackets back and forth to each other over line, towel, bench, chair, and net using forehands and backhands.
- In alley, service courts, backcourts.
- Play game with ball on 2 or 1 bounces.
- Score a point when opponent fails to make return, play to 4 points.

Summary

This chapter presents many activities for young beginners who have never been exposed to tennis or taken tennis lessons. Munchkin I begins with a description of a method of teaching called movement education. It is followed by simple juggling and then many important ball and racket skills. The skills are arranged in a logical progression to help children acquire what is needed to play tennis games of low organization presented in the next chapter.

Parents can help all of their players be successful when they are aware of how the movement characteristics of children differ from age to age, even group to group. The activities in this chapter can be modified, altered or presented in other sequences to suit the age, interests, and abilities of your children.

As children begin to manipulate the ball and racket more skillfully, incorporate the games found in Chapters 6 and 7 into your lessons. Simply end your session or lesson with a related game. They are fun and provide many excellent ways to actually "use" these Tennis Tasks. As children become more skillful, games like Munchkin Tennis offer a different level of excitement and enjoyment.

CHAPTER 6

MUNCHKIN II
LOW ORGANIZED GAMES

Munchkin II, games of low organization, is the second of four consecutive chapters that describe basic tennis activities for young children. The purpose of these games is to introduce the basic skills of tennis to first and second year Munchkins under the age of nine in an enjoyable way. When tennis is fun, children will continue to play tennis.

Games of low organization can involve a varying number of players. As such, they are quite suitable for tennis parties, picnics,

Tennis games have proven to be effective for retaining children in a Munchkin Tennis program.

birthday parties, and other gatherings of Munchkins at school, scouts and church. The games in Munchkin II can be used as culminating experiences for the movement activities and tennis tasks in the previous chapter. Lead-up games that more closely resemble "real" tennis are presented in the next chapter.

Tennis games

The tennis games in this chapter are well suited for young children. They can be made more difficult or challenging in six ways. They are:
1. increase the distance of players from net,
2. designate specific areas where the ball must land in order to complete the task or score,
3. add a locomotor movement to the task,
4. make more rapid or stronger feeds,
5. add spin to the feeds, and
6. require that two or more tasks be completed.

At all ages, the speed at which players must perform tasks changes the difficulty of games. Players who hit the ball at their own time and pace, as in serving, may be more accurate than when they are trying to finish before other players.

Tagging. Relay races are quite popular with all Munchkins. Put novelty in these events with added challenges. As they move to and from the target, require that they vary the tag or relay "touch." Alternatives include high fives, low fives, two hand slaps, and racket exchanges. Carrying and exchanging a tennis ball assures that all "tags" are made successfully. When mats and soft areas are available, tumbling rolls, stunts and jumps can be added.

Participation or elimination. Player elimination is a feature of many games. It may motivate some players to do well but elimination should not dominate the activities of young children for two reasons. First, the least skilled players who need the most playing time are usually among the first to be eliminated. Second, players learn very little waiting and watching. Total participation is the philosophy of Munchkin Tennis because it is fun. It also increases the speed at which learning occurs.

Winning and losing. Children learn from games. They enjoy playing even when winning and losing are not clearly defined or loudly proclaimed as is most evident in our traditional sports. They will eagerly play games such as Freeze and Defrost where the objective is to try selected tennis movement. While winning and losing are important elements in tennis, parents should see that total participation and the joy it produces receives primary emphasis.

The following games are for Munchkin II. In most cases, they are described on one page. The accompanying diagram illustrates how the activity can be conducted, including the position of parents. Games can be played on tennis courts, playgrounds, lawns, parking lots, driveways, in gymnasiums, exercise studios and in many other under-used areas not specifically designed for tennis. Modify or change these games in any way to make them more "playable" for your group or facility. Each game includes a description, variations, players needed, equipment and objectives.

1. Basketball Tennis

Description: Players form team lines behind the baseline facing the net. Each player bounces the ball forward with racket to a designated place on the court and hits the ball over the net. Tennis courts can be marked like a basketball court. Far shots are worth three points, closer shots two points and one point for shortest shots. Team with the most points after one, two or three rounds wins.

Variations: 1. Players hit ball from baseline, service line or corner. 2. Shot landing in backcourt is 3 points, alley is 2 points, frontcourt is 1 point. 3. Use only crosscourt shots.

Players: 3-6 players per team in relay formation with 2 teams per court.

Equipment: Tennis balls, rackets, court markings.

Objectives:
1. Racket control.
2. Hit the ball in a specific direction and to a specific area.

2. Beat the Clock

Description: Players form a straight line between baseline to net with a stack of balls behind baseline. First player puts a ball on racket and passes it to racket of next player in line without handling the ball. The last player in line at the net flips the ball over the net and runs to the baseline to get a ball. This player starts the next ball as every player moves up one position toward the net. Repeat this until all balls are over the net. First team seated in line wins.

Variations: 1. Game is over when all players return to starting position. 2. Hit forehand, backhand, or serve when at the net.

Players: 3-6 players per team in relay formation with 2 to 5 teams per court.

Equipment: Tennis balls, rackets.

Objectives:
1. Develop wrist and arm strength.
2. Racket and ball control.
3. Balance ball on racket.

3. Blow Out

Description: Players lay on stomach facing each other with hands under chins, and elbows out to the sides. Ball is placed between two lines (masking tape) or on a towel. On signal, players blow ping pong ball over line or into opponent to score a point. No hands permitted. Individual or team play.

Variations: 1. Play on table tops or benches. 2. Use window cleaner squirt bottles or detergent squeeze bottles filled with water.

Players: Singles, doubles or teams.

Equipment: Ping pong balls or balloons, masking tape or towel.

Objectives:
1. Move ball specific direction.
2. Respiratory exercise.

4. Bounce! Bounce! Bounce!

Description: Players are scattered randomly around the court, each with racket and ball. Players bounce ball with racket. When control is lost, player retrieves the ball and bounces it with the hand instead of racket. When he/she loses control again, player kneels and bounces ball. Finally sits and bounces ball. Players still bouncing ball with racket at final signal are winners and may receive special privilege like being first in line for next event.

Variations: 1. Bounce ball in air, or other combinations.

Players: Any number of players.

Equipment: Rackets, tennis balls.

Objectives:
1. Develop hand-eye coordination.
2. Racket and ball control.

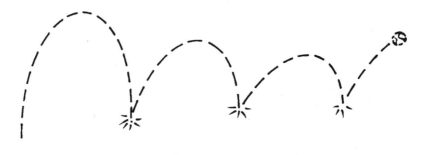

5. Bouncing and Moving

Description: Players move randomly around court, each with racket and ball. On command, they stop and execute a specific tennis task like grip, forehand or backhand stroke, ready position, jump racket handle, ups and downs, or skip as bounce ball. Resume moving on signal.

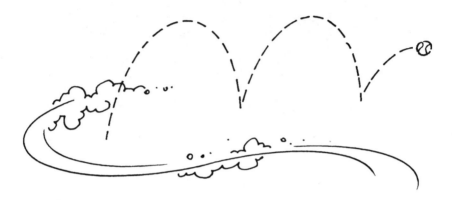

Variations: 1. Players move around the area using any of the 8 fundamental locomotor movements. They include: walk, run, skip, gallop, slide, jump, hop and leap. 2. Move around area in random order bouncing ball on ground or in air using locomotor movements on command.

Players: Any number.

Equipment: Rackets, tennis balls.

Objectives:
1. Racket and ball control.
2. Develop wrist and arm strength.
3. Listen, pay attention.

BOUNCING & MOVING

6. Bowling Tennis

Description: Tennis cans, painted white with stripes to look like bowling pins, are set up on one side of the net. Players get two shots from the other side of the net to knock down all the pins (cans). They can drop hit the ball with self-feeds or reduce the distance from the "pins" depending on skill level. Players have cards on which to keep their own score like bowling. Players receive one point for each pin felled and a strike when all 10 cans are felled on the first ball. Player or team with the highest score after 5 to 10 frames wins.

Variation: 1. Place a set of pins in each service court and practice the serve. 2. Place two sets of pins in each backcourt or near the baseline and have four teams hit groundstrokes from behind baseline.

Players: 3-5 players per team in relay formation with 2 to 4 teams per court.

Equipment: Tennis balls, rackets, tennis cans, scorecards. Use also quart milk or soft drink bottles with about one-half inch of sand in the bottom.

Objectives:
1. Self-feed to start play.
2. Hit a specific target.
3. Use groundstroke or serve with accuracy.

7. Box Tennis

Description: Players are in 2-6 groups of 3 each with one racket and 3 tennis balls. Of the players, 1 hits, 1 holds balls for hitter, 1 retrieves misses. Hitter is at the baseline with large container in service court. Each player in turn hits one ball from a self-feed into box on fly or bounce. Then next player hits. Take turns hitting, catching and retrieving.

Variations: 1. Hit until each gets one ball in box. 2. Team continues until their allotment of balls are in the box. 3. Various strokes required. 4. Increase distance between box and child to increase difficulty.

Players: 2-6 groups of 3 each.

Equipment: Rackets, tennis balls, large boxes.

Objectives:
1. Self-feed to start play.
2. Hit the ball over the net with control.

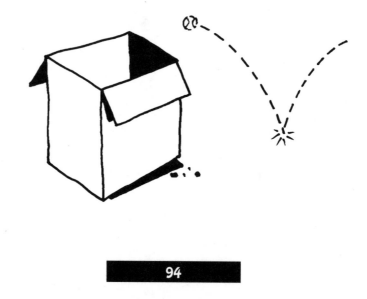

8. By the Numbers

Description: Players are positioned randomly about the court. On signal, toss and catch, dribble, or bounce ball on racket the correct number of times designated by leader.

Variation: 1. Add and subtract small numbers for young players. 2. Multiply and divide small numbers for older players.

Players: Any number.

Equipment: Rackets, tennis balls.

Objectives:
1. Develop hand-eye coordination.
2. Counting.
3. Stimulate mental functioning.

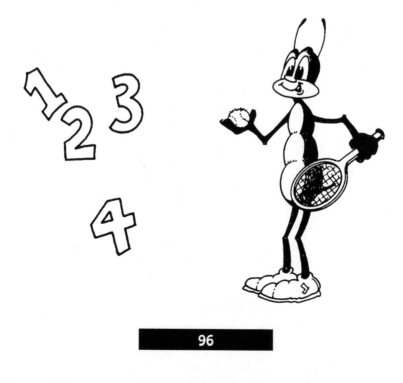

BY THE NUMBERS

9. Carry and Fetch

Description: Each player on relay team in turn carries a ball to a marker or bucket, places it on the ground, picks up another ball and returns, passing ball to teammate. If the ball falls off the racket, replace it, turn a complete circle, and continue. Winner is first team to complete rotation and be seated in line.

Variation: 1. Carry a variety of balls or other objects 2. More skilled players pick up ball without using hands.

Players: 2-8 relay teams of 3-5 players each.

Equipment: Rackets, tennis balls, markers.

Objectives:
1. Racket control
2. Develop hand-eye coordination

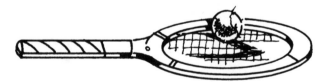

10. Caterpillar

Description: In relay formation, players pass ball back to next teammate. Last player in line runs to front of line with ball on racket. Lines "inch" forward as players change position. Complete a full rotation with players returning to their original position in line. See how many rotations can be made before ball is dropped.

Variations: 1. Use only one racket and ball per team. 2. Team that inches forward the most before dropping ball wins. 3. Pass ball or racket and ball between legs, over shoulder, alternate over and under. 4. Use larger balls for younger children.

Players: 2-8 relay teams of 3-5 players each.

Equipment: Rackets, tennis balls.

Objectives:
1. Racket control.
2. Develop hand-eye coordination.

11. Cats Have Two Lives

Description: Players, each with racket and 2 balls, are scattered randomly around the court. On the signal, players from team 1 move about the court bouncing ball in prescribed manner. Other team watches. When control of ball 1 is lost, start bouncing ball 2. When control of ball 2 is lost, player is dead and sits on the court. Teammates can revive dead players by giving them their extra ball. At signal, count the number of players who are alive. Now, second team goes. Team with most live players at the end wins.

Variations: 1. Bounce ball in air, or alternate ups and downs. 2. Both teams participate at same time, but on separate sides of net. 3. Players on same side of net tag opponents and receive one of their tennis balls. When both balls are gone, they are eliminated. Be seated.

Players: Any number of players on 2-6 teams.

Equipment: Rackets, tennis balls.

Objectives:
1. Racket and ball control.
2. Develop wrist and arm strength.
3. Evasive action.

12. Clean up your Room

Description: Players at each court are divided into 2 teams, one team at each baseline. Divide tennis balls evenly between teams. On signal, players from each team drop-hit balls across net. On next signal, players stop. All balls are retrieved and counted. Team with the fewest tennis balls on their side of net wins. Caution about racket safety.

Variations: 1. Use backhand or serve. 2. Partners drop ball for each other.

Players: 6-10 players per court.

Equipment: Rackets, tennis balls.

Objectives:
1. Self-feed to start play.
2. Hit the ball over the net with control.

13. Clear the Net

Description: Players form two or three teams behind baseline in relay formation facing net. Stack of balls at net in front of each team. Players run to net, in turn, pick up one ball and hit it over net using designated stroke. First team to make all their shots and be seated at baseline wins.

Variations: 1. Place on the court for the shot can change from baseline to service line to net in order to increase difficulty. 2. Hit forehand, backhand, or serve. 3. Use only one racket per team. 4. Dribble the ball to the net.

Players: 3-6 players per team in relay formation with 2 to 5 teams per court.

Equipment: Tennis balls, rackets.

Objectives: 1. Run fast and stop quickly. 2. Stroke ball across net with control.

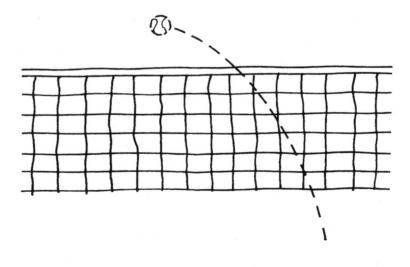

14. Crazy Catches

Description: Players line up on baseline in two teams. Instructor, on opposite side of the net, hits a ball to each player in turn flat or with varying amounts of top, side or backspin. Players catch the ball. Each team has a caught or missed basket in which to put balls. Team with the most balls in their caught basket wins.

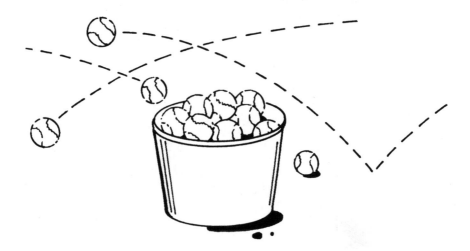

Variations: 1. Players shuffle or run to side to make catch. 2. Catch balls in bucket.

Players: 3-6 players per team in relay formation with 2 to 5 teams per court.

Equipment: Tennis balls, 2 baskets per team.

Objectives:
1. Develop hand-eye coordination.
2. Adjust for spin on the ball.

15. Crows and Cranes

Description: Players are divided into two groups in wave formation on lines facing each other. One group is crows, the other group is cranes. Leaders call out *Crrr...ows* or *Crrrr...anes*. The other group called becomes taggers and they chase the other group back to their home line. Those tagged join the other group and the game continues. Both groups must balance or bounce tennis balls during the chase. Use doubles sidelines on two adjacent tennis courts as starting lines with opposite doubles sidelines as home base.

Variations: 1. Players can do this with or without tennis rackets and balls. Players can carry the ball, bounce the ball by hand or use rackets.

Players: Group divided in half.

Equipment: Rackets, tennis balls.

Objectives: 1. Racket and ball control. 2. Listen, pay attention. 3. Fast reaction to signal.

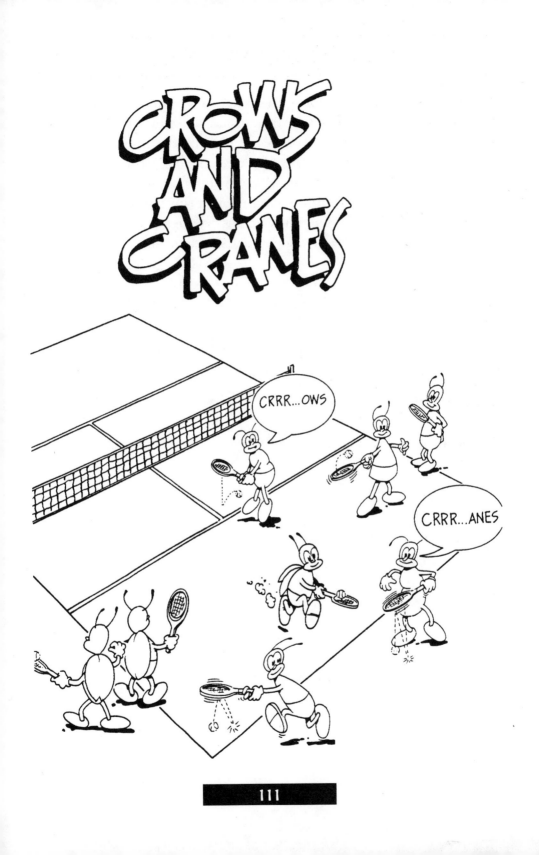

16. Dizzy Lizzy

Description: Players form lines of teams on the baseline facing the net. At the net there is a stack of balls, a marker and a racket for each team. The first player in line runs up to the marker, places the racket head on top of the marker, and places their forehead against the butt of the racket. Players then spin once around the marker, pick up one ball, and hit it over the net. Once the ball clears the net, player runs back across the baseline and the next player goes. The first team with all balls across the net wins.

Variations: 1. Require that ball be hit to specific area of court.

Players: 3-6 players per team in relay formation with 2 to 5 teams per court.

Equipment: Tennis balls, rackets, markers.

Objectives:
1. Hit the ball over the net.
2. Run fast and stop quickly.

17. Don't Break the Eggs

Description: Players form equal teams, half on each side of net in relay formation behind baseline. First player on each team has a racket. On signal, they pick up one egg (tennis ball) and place it on their racket. Carry egg to net and place it on partner's racket across net. Partner takes egg on racket and places it in basket at baseline. Tag next player in line at each baseline and repeat until all eggs are in the opposite baseline basket. Do not throw eggs. Place them carefully. Winner is first team completing relay and everyone seated behind full basket at baseline.

Variations: 1. Continue the relay until all eggs are returned to the original basket.

Players: 3-6 players per team on 2-6 teams.

Equipment: Rackets, tennis balls, buckets or hoops.

Objectives:
1. Racket and ball control.

18. Don't Drop the Egg

Description: Players form two teams in relay formation in each alley behind the baseline facing the net. Each team has a stack of balls. First two players put one ball between butt ends of their two rackets with arms extended. They race forward and drop the egg (ball) in the basket at the net. This pair returns to the baseline, makes a relay touch, and the next pair go in turn. Repeat this until all eggs are retrieved and in the basket. First team seated at the baseline wins.

Variation: 1. Partners take one egg to the basket and next pair retrieve it in shuttle relay formation. 2. Teams divided on each side of net. Partners take egg to net and pass it over net to teammates without using hands. Go to end of opposite line or return to same baseline.

Players: 3-6 players per team in relay or shuttle formation with 2-3 teams per court.

Equipment: Racket, tennis balls, basket.

Objectives:
1. Cooperation.
2. Have fun.

19. Easter Egg Hunt Contest

Description: Children are not permitted to see the courts before class. They are brought to the courts to find hidden colored tennis balls (or eggs) among the balls spread over the courts. Children line up at starting place, each with a basket. They bunny hop around the court looking for the colored balls. They must hop back to their basket and fill it. Balls can be old ones that parents fill with candy or that players trade for prizes or healthful snacks.

Variations: 1. See other holidays on page 285.

Players: Everyone, divided by age group.

Equipment: Old tennis balls, colored tennis balls, healthful snacks, basket for each child.

Objectives:
1. Find the colored balls.
2. Conditioning.

20. Follow the Leader

Description: Children form a single file behind parent, aid or more experienced player. Move around the court following lines performing different "tricks" or tennis tasks with racket and ball.

Variations: 1. Divide children into smaller groups once they are more familiar with tennis tasks and give others opportunity to lead. 2. Add variety by using 8 fundamental locomotor movements.

Players: Any number.

Equipment: Rackets, tennis balls.

Objectives: 1. Racket and ball control. 2. Learn parts of court. 3. Memory and remembering.

FOLLOW THE LEADER

21. Four Corners

Description: Place four rackets in the middle of the court with racket heads toward the four corners. Stack 1, 2 or 3 tennis balls per player at each corner in front of each player. Instructor starts the race in which each player in turn is to pick up one ball, run, and place ball on the racket. This is done until all balls from corner are stacked on racket. The first team to place all of their tennis balls on their racket and be seated in their corner wins.

Variation: 1. Last person returns the racket of balls to the corner.

Players: 3-6 players per team in relay formation with 2-3-4 teams per court.

Equipment: Tennis balls, rackets.

Objectives:
1. Speed, agility and rapid change of direction.
2. Bend knees to retrieve low balls.

FOUR CORNERS

22. Four Corners Relay

Description: Players form four teams in relay formation inside each corner of the court, facing out. At the signal, players run around outside boundary of the tennis court, each returning to their starting position. Tag the next player in line and repeat the circuit. Relay is complete when each player runs and all are seated inside the court.

Variations: 1. Carry one or more tennis balls. 2. Carry balls on rackets. 3. Dribble tennis balls. 4. Carry or dribble other types of balls. 5. Use any of the 8 fundamental locomotor movements to move around the court.

Players: 3-6 players per team in relay formation with 2-4 teams per court.

Equipment: None or rackets, tennis balls.

Objectives:
1. Improve speed and endurance.

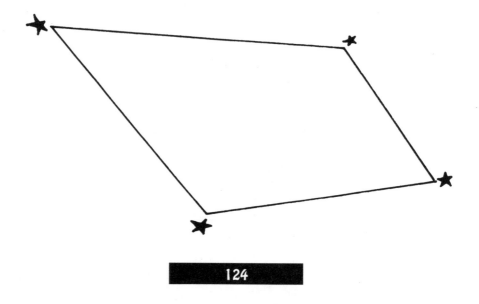

23. Freeze and Defrost

Description: Players are scattered randomly around the court, each with racket and ball. They move about the court bouncing the ball with their racket on the court. When they lose control of the ball, they retrieve it, then freeze, but continue the specified ball action. They may resume moving (defrosted) when touched by a defrosted player.

Variations: 1. Bounce ball in air, or other combinations. 2. Players divided into 2-5 teams. Frozen (stationary) players are defrosted when tagged by teammate.

Players: Any number of players; or 3-6 players per team on 2-6 teams.

Equipment: Rackets, tennis balls.

Objectives:
1. Watch the ball.
2. Racket and ball control.

24. Golf Tennis

Description: Players form two lines on baseline. A marker and stack of balls on a racket are placed in front of each team. First players run forward, place a ball on a marker. Players then hit the ball with a golf swing into the net. Players retrieve the ball at the net and hit it over the net. Players run back to their team, give racket to the next golfer, who repeats the task. The first team with all balls hit over the net and all players sitting in a line at the baseline wins.

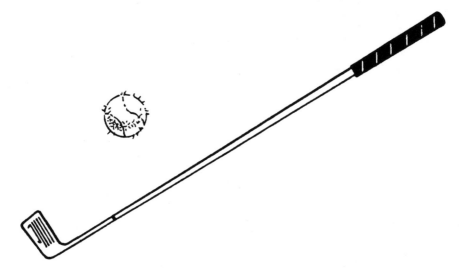

Variations: 1. Hit ball over net into specific area.

Players: 3-6 players per team in relay formation with 2 to 5 teams per court.

Equipment: Tennis balls, rackets, markers.

Objectives:
1. Watch the ball.
2. Hit ball over the net.
3. Run fast, stop quickly and change direction.

25. Grips and Stances

Description: Rackets are scattered around the court. Players move about court using any of eight fundamental locomotor movements. At signal, players find their racket and take tennis grip or stance called by instructor. Instructor tags as many players as possible before they find their racket and complete task. Win point by getting in position without being tagged. Winners are first players with four points.

Variations: 1. One or more players are "it." 2. See "Munchkin Sez..."

Players: Any number.

Equipment: Rackets, tennis balls.

Objectives: 1. Learn grips and stances. 2. Memory and remembering.

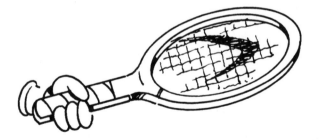

26. Hickery Dickery Dock

Description: Players form 2-6 equal teams of clocks and mice. Clock team, each with racket, are arranged around the court in circles of 3-6 players forming a clock. Players face inward and, in order, drop-bounce ball around the circle on their rackets. Other team is mice. They run, in shuttle relay formation, up and down the clock from one marker to the other. When the ball gets back to starting place, 12 o'clock, the mice stop running. Count the number of runs mice are able to make. Trade positions. Team with the most runs up and down the clock wins. Caution players about racket safety.

Variations: 1. Bounce ball in air, or other combinations. 2. Make 2-3 clock revolutions.

Players: 3-6 players per team on 2-6 teams.

Equipment: Rackets, tennis balls, markers.

Objectives:
1. Hand-eye coordination.
2. Racket and ball control.
3. Improve speed and endurance.

27. High Hurdles

Description: Players form two or three teams in relay formation behind baseline facing net. Two rows of markers, with a racket atop each pair, are lined up toward the net in front of each team. Each player, in turn, carries a ball on racket, runs, hops over each hurdle and returns to baseline. First team to complete course and be seated at baseline wins.

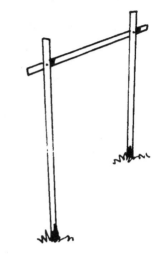

Safety Note: Remind players to jump high to clear the hurdles.

Variations: 1. Use only one racket per team and pass racket. 2. Player who loses ball must start over. 3. Player who loses ball must fetch it and perform a tennis task (e.g., two-foot agility hop over racket handle 4 times) before continuing the race. 4. Hit forehand, backhand, or serve when reach net. 5. Place pairs of tennis rackets (flat or on edge), balls or jump ropes spaced apart on the court as long jump hurdles.

Players: 3-6 players per team in relay formation with 2 to 3 teams per court.

Equipment: Tennis balls, rackets, 6-8 markers per team.

Objectives:
1. Develop leg strength and speed.
2. Balance ball on racket.

28. History Drill

Description: Players form single file formation behind the baseline facing net. Instructor at opposite baseline hits ball to player who returns it. Player continues to rally ball with parent as many times as possible. When player fails to make a return, another moves in as other children say: "You're history!"

Variations: 1. Play the ball to backhand only, or alternate forehands and backhands. 2. Play as service court game using blocks, short bumps and volleys.

Players: 3-6 players per court.

Equipment: Racket, tennis balls, tennis tube or basket.

Objectives:
1. Move to the ball.
2. Hit ball with control, not power.
3. Move quickly with racket control.
4. Use strokes with accuracy.
5. Court position and coverage.
6. Use skills in game situation.
7. Consistency.

Source: John Weil, Cincinnati, Ohio.

29. Hockey Tennis

Description: A portion of net is designated a goal with tennis rackets standing on end or markers 4' to 8' apart. Player (goalkeeper) stands with back to net. Instructor drop-hits 5 tennis balls at players attempting to hit ball into goal. Players rotate rapidly in and out of goal stopping shots on goal using specified ground-strokes or volley. Player is out when the parent scores 5 points. If last person has had fewer turns than others, player must go against the parent. This player wins if the parent does not score.

Variations: 1. Player with the fewest goals allowed is the winner. 2. Players push ball with racket attempting to score against others who take turns in goal.

Players: 3-10 players per parent.

Equipment: Tennis balls, rackets, markers.

Objectives: 1. Develop quick reaction to ball.

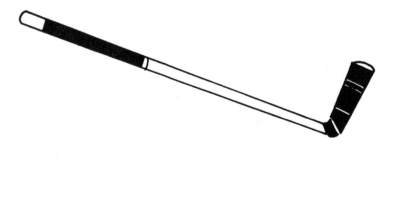

30. Hot Potato

Description: Players form circles on the court. Each circle is a team. Players pass a tennis ball from one racket to the next without handling or dropping the ball. Winner is the team that passes the hot potato around the circle one, two or three times or the most times in a given amount of time.

Variations: 1. Use only one racket per team and pass racket. 2. Player who has ball on their racket at "stop" signal must perform a tennis task (e.g., 10 ups and downs) before returning to hot potato race. 3. For advanced players, bounce ball from one player to next with or without allowing ball to hit ground. 4. Pass two or more balls, a variety of balls, or other objects around circle.

Players: 3-8 players per team in circle formation with 2 to 5 teams per court. 1 or 2 large circles.

Equipment: Tennis balls, rackets.

Objectives:
1. Develop wrist and arm strength.
2. Balance ball on racket.
3. Fast reaction to ball.

31. Hula Tennis

Description: Players form lines of teams on the baseline facing the net. Hula hoops (2-4) are placed in a straight line in front of each team with a stack of balls and racket at the net. Players hop to the net through each hula hoop. At the net, pick up a ball and racket and hit ball over the net. Place racket by the stack and return to baseline hopping through each hoop.

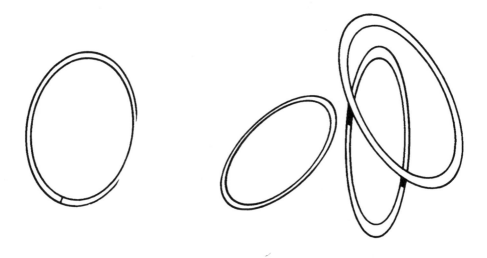

Variations: 1. Place on the court from which to hit can change from net to service line to baseline in order to increase difficulty. 2. Hit forehand, backhand or serve.

Players: 3-6 players per team in relay formation with 2 to 5 teams per court.

Equipment: Tennis balls, rackets, hula hoops.

Objectives:
1. Run fast and stop quickly.
2. Hit ball over net with control.

32. Ice Cream Cone Contest

Description: Players form a circle around the parent. Hold racket upside down at end of handle with head toward court. Place a ball on end of handle. Instructor blows a whistle and players move to commands of parent. Last person to have the ice cream (ball) fall off their ice cream cone (racket) wins.

Variations: 1. Players run or shuffle around in a circle. 2. Play follow the leader. 3. Perform stunts like high fives, jump markers the leader or other players call.

Players: 6-20 players in circle formation with one parent per group.

Equipment: Racket, tennis balls, whistle.

Objectives:
1. Develop wrist strength and balance.
2. Listen, pay attention.

33. Infinity Tennis

Description: Partners scattered randomly over area. See which pair can control ball longest by bouncing ball back and forth. Use forehand or backhand against wall, over line, towel, bench, chair or net. Partners sit when they lose control of ball. Last pair standing wins.

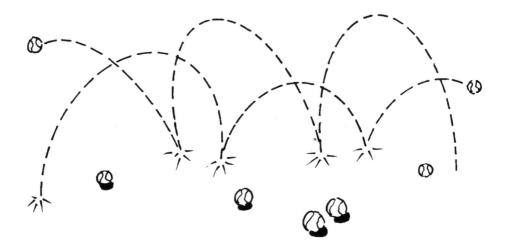

Variations: 1. Players may restart one or two times without penalty using one of the ball pick-up skills. 2. Players who lose control of ball join another group and continue. 3. Larger group keeps two or more tennis balls in play on one court at same time.

Players: Partners.

Equipment: Rackets, tennis balls.

Objectives:
1. Consistency.
2. Develop racket control.
3. Move to the ball.

34. Keep it Up

Description: Players are in circles about the court. One player has a beach ball. Players in each circle hit ball into the air keeping it up. See which team can keep the ball in the air longest.

Variations: 1. Can also be played with different kinds of rackets. Issue safety reminders. 2. Allow one bounce between hits if needed. 3. Count the number of hits in time allotted. 4. Use two balls and larger groups for older players.

Players: Groups of 3-5.

Equipment: Beach balls.

Objectives:
1. Develop hand-eye coordination.
2. Track ball in flight
3. Have fun.

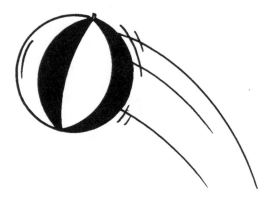

35. Kick the Bucket

Description: Players form two teams in relay formation behind the baseline facing the net. Parent stands at the service line "T" with some balls and a plastic bucket or tennis ball can for each team. A racket is placed near the net for each team. Parent says "go" and first player on each team runs forward and picks up their bucket. Parent feeds a ball in the air to each player. Players catch one ball in the bucket, run to the net, place the bucket down, kick the bucket, pick up the ball, take a racket placed near the net and hit the ball over the net. First team to have all players catch a ball, hit it over the net and be seated at baseline wins.

Variations: 1. Players hit forehand, backhand or serve.

Players: 3-6 players per team in relay formation with 2 teams per court.

Equipment: Tennis balls, plastic buckets or tennis ball cans, tennis racket for each team.

Objectives:
1. Develop hand-eye coordination.
2. Track ball in flight.
3. Move to the ball.

36. Knock it Off

Description. Players form two equal teams, one on each side of net. Place one basketball (or other ball) on tennis ball can in each backcourt. Players drop-hit forehands across net from behind service line or baseline. Object is to knock ball off can.

Variations: 1. Throw tennis balls to practice overhand serve motion. 2. Drop-hit backhands. 3. Serve from service line, any place in backcourt, or baseline. 4. Place any number of tennis ball cans in the service court or backcourt. Hit until one team knocks all balls off can. 5. With ball machine, players hit in turn until time is up. Others retrieve balls, fill machine, then take their turn.

Players: 3-6 per team, 2 teams per court.

Equipment: Rackets, basketballs or tennis balls, tennis ball cans. Ball machine too.

Objectives:
1. Hit a specific target or area.
2. Learn overhand throwing motion for serve.

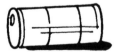

37. Mad Hatter

Description: Players scattered randomly around court, each with racket and ball, one or more players wear funny hats or caps. Players move about court bouncing ball with racket in prescribed manner. Player(s) with hat attempts to tag players without hats. Those without hats avoid tag. Lose control of ball while being chased and you become it and wear hat.

Variations: 1. Bounce ball in air, or other combinations. 2. Form relay teams and exchange hat with teammates. 3. Players without hats try to get hats.

Players: Any number of players; or 3-6 players per team on 2-6 teams.

Equipment: Rackets, tennis balls, hats or caps.

Objectives:
1. Racket and ball control.
2. Evasive action to move away from the ball.

38. Mad Hatter - full page illustration

38. Munchkin Relay

Description: Players form two teams in relay formation in each alley behind the baseline facing the net. Place 3 to 5 rackets on edge spaced evenly apart in each alley on the other side of the net. Players, in turn, run to the net and bunny hop over each racket. Circle the court and return to starting position. Next player may go when relay touch (e.g., high five) is made. First team to complete the circuit and be seated at baseline wins.

Variations: 1. Use each of the eight fundamental locomotor movements to circle the court. They are: walk, run, skip, gallop, slide, jump, hop and leap. 2. Place pairs of tennis rackets (flat or on edge), balls or jump ropes spaced apart in alleys as long jump hurdles.

Safety Note: Caution players to jump vigorously to clear hurdles.

Players: 3-6 players per team in relay formation with 2 teams per court.

Equipment: 3-6 markers/team, tennis rackets.

Objectives:
1. Develop leg strength and power.
2. Improve speed and endurance.

39. Munchkin Sez . . .

Description. Players stand around the court, each with racket and ball. On the command "Munchkin Sez…," they execute a specific tennis task like grip, forehand or backhand stroke, ready position, jump racket handle, ups and downs, or bounce ball. Hold position until next command. Players do not move when "Munchkin Sez…" does not start the command. Those who move must go to side and perform some tennis task.

Variations: 1. Execute commands while moving around the court in random pattern. 2. Move using 8 fundamental locomotor movements.

Players: Any number of players.

Equipment: Rackets, tennis balls.

Objectives:
1. Racket and ball control.
2. Listen, pay attention.
3 Memory and remembering.

40. Musical Chairs

Description: Chairs are placed on the court in a small circle with backs of chairs together. Players form a circle around chairs with a ball on their racket. Players begin walking around chairs while parent plays a tape recorder or sings. When music stops, players must sit in empty chairs while keeping ball on their racket. Player who does not get to a chair is eliminated. Remove one chair and repeat. Repeat until there are two players and one chair left. Last player to have a seat wins.

Variations: 1. Parent can use portable radio or whistle rather than tape recorder. 2. Use rackets standing on end in a circle rather than chairs. 3. Rather than eliminate players, remove chairs and players sit on fewer and fewer chairs until all are on one chair. Version 3 is a great ice breaker.

Players: 6-20 players in circle formation with one parent per group.

Equipment: Racket, tennis balls, chairs, tape recorder, music.

Objectives:
1. Move quickly while maintaining control of racket.
2. Have fun.

41. Old MacDonald

Description: Players spread about court with racket. Follow the leader singing "Old MacDonald" using words for tennis. Act out each verse.

Old MacDonald had a tennis court. E-I-E-I-O.
And on his court he had a forehand. E-I-E-I-O.
With a forehand here, forehand there, here a forehand, there a forehand, everywhere a forehand.
Old MacDonald had a tennis court. E-I-E-I-O.

Other verses:
On his court he had a backhand. E-I-E-I-O.
On his court he had a serve. E-I-E-I-O.
On his court he had a volley. E-I-E-I-O.
On his court he had an overhead. E-I-E-I-O.
On his court he had a forehand and backhand. E-I-E-I-O.
On his court he had a serve and volley. E-I-E-I-O.

Variations: 1. Sing "Old MacDonald" using strokes in combination to move and practice a combination of strokes used in tennis. 2. Sing to stretching or fitness exercises.

Players: Group.

Equipment: Rackets.

Objectives:
1. Listen, pay attention.
2. Learn grip and stance.
3. Develop footwork.
4. Cooperation.

42. On Target

Description: Players, in groups of 2-4, start 5 steps from wall. Bounce ball with self-feed forehand and hit target on wall. Back up one more step with each hit, 6 steps and repeat, 7 steps, 8 steps. Continue until miss target. Other players retrieve balls and hand them to hitter. Then next person in same group takes their turn. Player from each group who gets most steps from wall wins.

Variations: 1. Use backhand or serve. 2. Lay towels or boxes on court and hit target.

Players: Groups of 2-4 players.

Equipment: Rackets, tennis balls, wall, targets.

Objectives:
1. Hit a specific target.
2. Develop racket control.
3. Self-feed to start play.

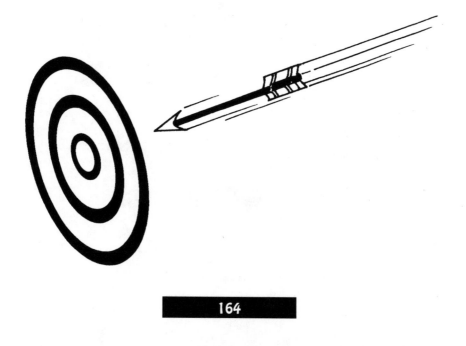

43. Perpetual Motion

Description: Players are divided into two groups and scattered about their side of court in random order with a ball or a ball and racket in front of them on court. On signal, players are to move ball non-stop in the designated manner. Roll it. Dribble it. Bounce it. When the leader spots a ball not moving, their group loses one point. First team to lose all five points loses the game.

Variations: 1. Players can move or bounce the ball by foot, hand or racket.

Players: Group divided in half.

Equipment: Rackets, tennis balls.

Objectives:
1. Develop hand-eye coordination.
2. Racket and ball control.

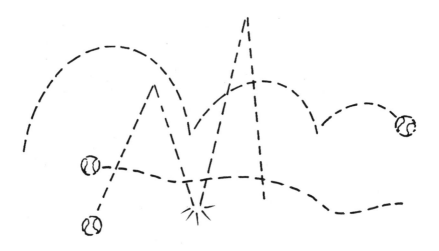

PERPETUAL MOTION

44. Polar Tennis

Description: Players are divided into hitting team in single file and fielding team scattered about the playing area. First player on hitting team (A) hits, kicks or throws the ball and begins circling teammates. Fielding players (B) retrieve the ball. All players on fielding team then line up in single file behind person with ball. Ball is passed overhead to end of fielding line where the last player brings the ball to the front of the line, sits and shouts, "Freeze." Hitting team scores a point for each time the hitter circles teammates. Balls hit over the court fences are outs.

Variations: 1. Also called Polar Baseball. 2. Use entire court area. 3. Use a variety of balls.

Players: Two teams.

Equipment: Variety of balls, rackets.

Objectives:
1. Hitting with force.
2. Quick reaction to ball.
3. Develop hand-eye coordination.
4. Teamwork.

POLAR TENNIS

45. Popcorn

Description: Players, each with racket, are arranged around the court in circles of 3-6 players. Players face inward and, in order, bounce ball around the circle on their rackets without allowing ball to touch the ground. Count the hits. Team with the most popcorn (total hits) at the signal wins.

Safety Note: Caution players about racket safety.

Variations: 1. Bounce ball on ground, or other combinations. 2. Score returns to zero when miss ball or control is lost. 3. Bounce the ball around the circle in any order. 4. Face out rather than in. 5. Form large circle and bounce ball on ground in the center as players run in and out of circle in turn. 6. Form shuttle relay teams on each side of net. See Around The World. 7. Use wall bounces when rebound surface is available.

Players: 3-6 players per team on 2-6 teams.

Equipment: Rackets, tennis balls.

Objectives:
1. Racket and ball control.
2. Move to the ball.
3. Cooperate.

POPCORN

46. Pop It Up and Run

Description: Players form two or three teams behind baseline facing net. Each team has one ball. First player pops ball up and runs around a marker in service court while letting ball bounce once. Same player pops it up again while returning to baseline. Then each player in turn pops it up 2 times while running to target and back to baseline. First team to complete relay wins.

Variations: 1. Use different types of balls.

Players: 3-6 players per team in relay formation with 2-3 teams per court.

Equipment: Tennis balls, rackets.

Objectives:
1. Track ball in flight.
2. Move to the ball.
3. Move quickly with racket control.
4. Hit with control, not power.

47. Racket Relay

Description: Players line up in relay formation outside singles or doubles sideline facing opposite sideline. Rackets for each team are placed in line along center service line from net to baseline or baseline to baseline. On signal, first player from each team races forward, picks up their team racket, races around marker on the opposite sideline, returns and places team racket back on center service line. Continue to race back to team. Tag next player who repeats relay. Winner is first team completing relay and seated behind sideline. Do not throw rackets. Place them carefully.

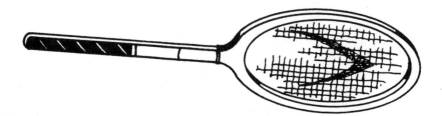

Variations: 1. First player brings racket back to next player in line. Next player puts racket back on center service line as he/she returns from other sideline. 2. Stand racket on end before moving on. 3. Each player carries the same racket. 4. Move using tennis side shuffle step or backward running.

Players: 3-6 players per team on 2-6 teams.

Equipment: Rackets, markers.

Objectives:
1. Teamwork.
2. Speed, agility and rapid change of direction.
3. Bend knees to receive low balls or shots.

48. Red Light! Green Light!

Description: All players line up two steps behind the baseline facing the net with a ball on their racket. Parent on the other side of the net stands back to the players and starts counting loudly: "One, two, three, Red Light!" Then the parent turns to face the players. While leader counts, the players walk or run to the net with the ball on their racket. They must stop moving when the parent says Red Light and turns around. On "Green Light," children may move forward again. From where they finally stop, players must drop and hit the ball over the net for a point. The closer the players get to the net, the easier it is to score. Players caught moving must hit a shot of the parent's choice. The player with the most points wins.

Variations: 1. Players caught moving must hit a more difficult shot of parent's choice. 2. Players must hit the ball into a designated part of the court to score. 3. Place one-half of the players on each baseline. 4. Players caught moving return to baseline and are eliminated.

Players: 10-12 players. Up to 10 players per team, 2 teams per court.

Equipment: Tennis balls, rackets.

Objectives:
1. Listen, pay attention.
2. Racket and ball control.
3. Move quickly with racket control.
4. Hit the ball over the net with control.

49. Sandwich Tennis

Description: Players form two teams in relay formation behind baseline facing net. Each team has a stack of balls. First two players put one ball between their two rackets, race forward and flip the ball over the net. Next pair may go when both relay touches (e.g., high five) are made. First team to complete circuit and be seated at baseline wins.

Variations: 1. Partners hold rackets horizontally (flat) or vertically (up). 2. Carry 2-3 tennis balls between rackets. 3. Teams divided on each side of net. Partners take ball to net and pass it over net to next pair without using hands. Go to end of opposite line or return to same baseline. 4. Hands not permitted to touch tennis balls.

Players: 2-6 players per team in relay formation with 2-3 teams per court.

Equipment: Rackets, tennis balls.

Objectives:
1. Racket control.
2. Cooperation.
3. Have fun.

50. Scoop and Scoot

Description: Players form two teams in relay formation behind the baseline facing the net. A chaser from each team is on the opposite side of the net. A stack of balls and one racket are placed at the net for each team. The first player runs to the stack, takes one ball, and hits it over the net very softly to the chaser who has a basket or tennis tube. The chaser retrieves the ball and puts it in the basket. The chaser puts the basket down and runs to the baseline with the other players and the next player goes. The player who hits the ball over the net to the chaser places the racket near the stack, crosses around the net, and becomes the new chaser. The first team with all balls in the basket and seated at the baseline wins.

Variations: 1. Players hit forehand, backhand or serve.

Players: 3-6 players per team in relay formation with 2 teams per court.

Equipment: Rackets, tennis balls, basket or tennis tube.

Objectives:
1. Racket control for soft net shot.
2. Cooperation.
3. Fast reaction to the ball, reflex action.
4. Speed, agility and rapid change of direction.

51. Sharks

Description: Players are scattered about the area in groups of four. Three players join hands to form a shark cage. A scuba diver gets in each cage with a camera (tennis ball). On signal, all players raise their hands and divers change cages while one player, the shark, tries to capture (tag) one person. Players cannot be captured when in cages. Players must bounce, dribble, toss and catch or perform other tasks with their ball as they change cages. Players may not return to the same cage nor enter cage without their camera. Person tagged trades places with shark. Change places frequently so each member of cage can be a diver.

Variations: 1. Use a variety of balls. Also called Squirrels in the Trees.

Players: Groups of 4 with one inside circle.

Equipment: Variety of balls.

Objectives:
1. Develop hand-eye coordination.
2. Speed, agility and rapid change of direction.

52. Shooting Gallery

Description: Similar to Humpty Dumpty except the purpose is to knock the tennis ball cans off the benches. Players at each court are divided into 2 teams, one behind each baseline. Place a row of 10-20 tennis ball cans on benches between two teams. Each player has 2 tennis balls. Players from the first team hit ball #1 over the wall (bench) and then ball #2. Knock tennis ball cans off the bench. Other team retrieves balls, sets tennis ball cans back on the wall, and returns to baseline. On signal, this team hits ball #1 and ball #2 over the wall. Award a team point for each can felled after each round. Repeat 2-4 rounds. Team with most points wins.

Variations: 1. Use backhand or serve. 2. Place tennis ball cans in service courts to develop serve. 3. Place tennis ball cans in backcourt to work on depth. 4. Place cans on benches between courts.

Players: 12-20 players per court, go in waves.

Equipment: Rackets, tennis balls, tennis ball cans, benches.

Objectives:
1. Racket and ball control.
2. Hit a specific target or area.

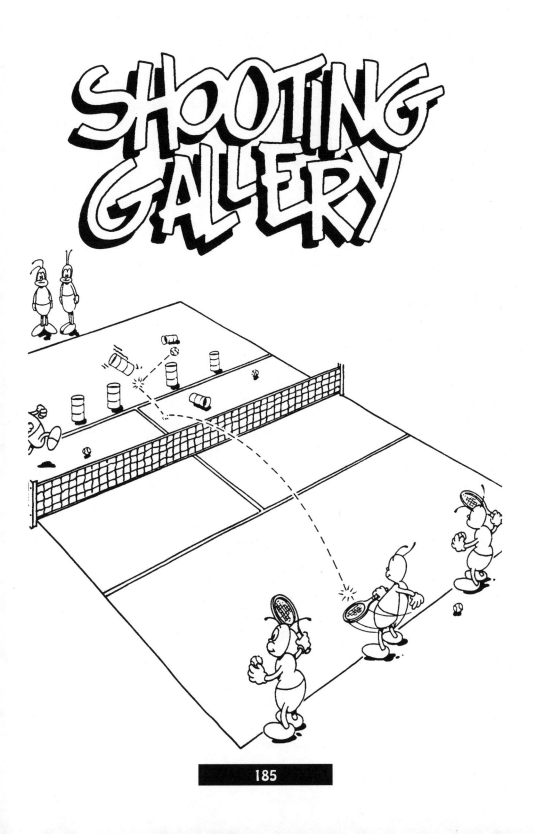

53. Show Time

Description: Players move randomly around the court, each with racket and ball. On command, they stop or execute a specific tennis task like grip, forehand, backhand stroke, serve, ready position, jump racket handle, ups and downs, or skip as they bounce ball. Resume moving on signal.

Variations: 1. Move using 8 fundamental locomotor movements. 2. See "Munchkin Sez..." on page 158.

Players: Any number of players.

Equipment: Rackets, tennis balls.

Objectives:
1. Learn grip and stance.
2. Racket and ball control.
3. Listen, pay attention.

54. Sprint Like the Stars

Description: Players form two teams behind the baseline facing the net. Parent is across the net at the service line or baseline to increase level of difficulty. Players run to the net on signal. First one there hits a volley over the net and returns to baseline. Parent feeds players from each team alternately or single player at the net while next player sprints forward. First team to make all their volleys and be seated wins.

Variations: 1. Use only one racket per team. 2. Add a second stroke like approach shot followed by volley. 3. Sprint around the court after successful volley. 4. Run around all the courts after successful volley.

Players: 3-6 players per team in relay formation with 2 teams per court.

Equipment: Tennis balls, rackets.

Objectives:
1. Run fast and stop quickly.
2. Watch the ball.
3. Combination movement and stroke.

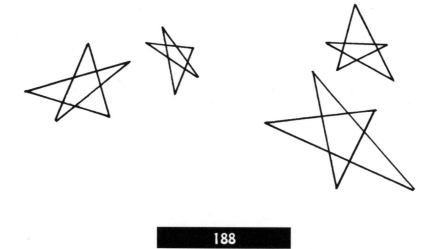

55. Team Toss

Description: Players are scattered about the area in random order. Leader tosses a ball to one player who tosses it to another until each player has received the ball with no repeats. Remember who the ball was tossed to each time and follow that order. Repeat. Start a second ball, third ball. See how many balls the group can send at one time.

Variations: 1. Use game as an ice breaker. Say your name and player to whom ball is passed. 2. Use a variety of balls. 3. Mix two groups of players together but toss only to your group.

Players: One or two groups, any size.

Equipment: Tennis balls or a variety of balls.

Objectives:
1. Develop hand-eye coordination.
2. Track ball in flight.
3. Fast reaction to ball.
4. Memory and remembering.

56. Tennis Ball Tag

Description: Players are positioned randomly about court and cannot move. One player has a tennis ball. Person who is "it" chases player with ball in hand. Player with ball may hand it to any other player at any time. Player who receives the ball must take the ball. Others may not move. When person with ball is tagged, he or she becomes it. "It" must count to four (15, 30, 40 game) before chasing anyone.

Variation: 1. Use two or three balls. 2. Make two or three players "it."

Players: Any number.

Equipment: Tennis balls, variety of balls.

Objectives:
1. Improve speed and endurance.
2. Run fast, stop quickly and change direction.
3. Learn tennis scoring system.

57. Tennis Bucket Brigade

Description: Players on teams line up one behind another in relay formation. There is basket or stack of balls at one end of the line and empty basket at other end. First player on each team puts a ball on racket and passes it to next person in line with a drop-bounce. Each ball is passed this way (bucket brigade) until all balls are in other basket. First team to complete task and be seated in line wins.

Variations: 1. Place players far apart, baseline to baseline, so ball must be hit accurately from one player to the next. 2. Pass balls with air bounce. Players: 3-6 players on 2-6 teams per court.

Equipment: Rackets, tennis balls, baskets.

Objectives:
1. Racket and ball control.
2. Track ball in flight.

58. Tennis Marathon

Description: Players are in groups of 3-5 with one racket and one ball. Player 1 repeatedly bounces ball off wall. Player 2 counts hits. Player 3 runs one lap around the court. Count the number of wall hits or partner bumps while player runs. Each player takes a turn running. Player with most hits while teammates run, wins.

Variations: 1. Use forehand, backhand or serve. 2. Bounce ball on court, in air or across net with partner.

Players: Groups of 3-5 players.

Equipment: Rackets, tennis balls, wall.

Objectives:
1. Watch the ball.
2. Hit ball in specific direction.
3. Improve conditioning.

59. Tennis "Tube Basket" Race

Description: Players form teams in relay formation behind the baseline facing the net. Each team has a tennis tube, basket or racket at the baseline and stack of balls at the net. First player runs to the net, picks up three balls, returns to baseline, and passes the tube to the next player in line. Repeat this until all balls are retrieved. First team seated at the baseline wins.

Variation: 1. Return tennis balls on racket and put them in a basket. 2. Return all tennis balls on the racket. 3. Scatter balls about the court. Each team picks up as many balls as possible — 1, 2 or 3 balls per person.

Players: 3-6 players per team in relay formation with 2-5 teams per court.

Equipment: Racket, tennis balls, tennis tube or basket.

Objectives:
1. Develop arm and wrist strength.
2. Teamwork.
3. Move quickly with racket control.

60. Tennis Volleyball

Description: Players form teams on each side of the net, 2 to 6 per side. Players hit the ball back and forth across the net. It must go upward when crossing the net. Ball can be played on one or more bounces and can be hit any number of times on each side of the net. Score four-point games as in tennis or play 15-point games as in volleyball.

Variations: 1. Younger children can play the ball until it stops rolling. 2. Move toward one-bounce rule as players develop more skill. 3. Use volleyball or beach ball to introduce the game.

Players: 3-6 players per team with 2 teams per court.

Equipment: Rackets, tennis ball, volleyball, beach ball.

Objectives:
1. Develop racket and ball control.
2. Move to the ball.
3. Develop footwork.

61. Triple Decker Sandwich

Description: This game is like Sandwich Tennis with the addition of a third player. Players form two teams in relay formation behind baseline facing the net. Each team has a stack of balls. First three players put two balls between their three rackets, race forward and flip the ball over the net. Next threesome may go when all relay touches (e.g., high five) are made. First team to complete the circuit and be seated at the baseline wins.

Variations: 1. Hold rackets vertically or horizontally. 2. Carry 2-3 tennis balls between each racket. 3. Teams divided on each side of net. Partners take balls to net and pass it over net to next threesome without using hands. Go to end of opposite line or return to same baseline. 4. Hands not permitted to touch tennis balls.

Players: 3-6 players per team in relay formation with 2 teams per court.

Equipment: Rackets, tennis balls.

Objectives:
1. Racket control.
2. Cooperation.
3. Have fun.

TRIPLE DECKER SANDWICH

62. Ups and Downs

Description: Players spaced randomly around the court, each with one tennis ball and racket. Bounce ball on the court and in the air a variety of ways. For example: 1. bounce ball on court using forehand side of racket; backhand side. 2. bounce ball in air using backhand side of racket; forehand side. 3. bounce ball on court where 2 lines meet using forehand side of racket. 4. alternate ups and downs. 5. alternate sides of racket in air. 6. use edge of racket. 7. Follow The Leader, a good warm-up to start class.

Variations: 1. To add variety to later lessons, incorporate spelling and math tables into counting hits. Make 20 taps counting by 2's, 30 hits counting by 3's, 100 hits counting by 5's, 99 hits counting by 11's, 144 hits counting by 12's. 2. For spelling, recite alphabet, spell your name, Munchkin Tennis and many other tennis words. 3. Repeat as a partner activity.

Players: Any number over the court.

Equipment: Tennis racket, ball for each.

Objectives:
1. Develop hand-eye coordination.
2. Develop wrist and arm strength.
3. Develop racket and ball control.
4. Provide home practice activity.

UPS & DOWNS

63. Volley Spin Race

Description: Players form two teams behind the baseline facing the net. Parent is across the net. First two players run to the net, make a volley, spin 360 degrees, and receive a second volley feed from the parent. When both volleys are successfully completed, players return to the baseline and the next player follows in turn. First team to make all their volleys and be seated wins.

Variations: 1. Take one forehand and one backhand volley. 2. Require that volley go into backcourt. 3. Plays shuffle from one side of net to other taking one volley in each service court.

Players: 3-6 players per team in relay formation with 2 teams per court.

Equipment: Tennis balls, rackets.

Objectives:
1. Run fast and stop quickly.
2. Stop and volley.

64. Volley Time

Description: Players are divided into 2-4 teams of 3-5 players. One team goes to the net. Other players each have two tennis balls and stand at the service line. On signal, the first group of feeders toss balls underhand to net players who attempt to block each toss with a volley. Each team volleys in turn. Award 1 point for each volley returned across the net. Distance between players depends on skill level and throwing accuracy.

Safety Note: Players are to toss their balls to the same person and only when "their" volleyer is ready and looking.

Variations: 1. Tossers can stand anywhere between service line and baseline. 2. Volleys can be made from either side of the net. 3. Position blockers in front of the net, prevent low bounces from getting through and hitting the net.

Players: 3-5 players on 2-4 teams per court.

Equipment: Rackets, tennis balls.

Objectives:
1. Racket and ball control.
2. Fast reaction to the ball, reflex action.

65. Wacky Knees

Description: Players form lines of teams on the baseline facing the net. Tennis balls are stacked at the service line and a tennis racket is placed at the net in front of each team. Players run in turn to the stack, pick up one ball, place it between their knees, and run to the net. At the net, they pick up a racket, drop the ball and hit it over the net. Next player may go when relay touch (e.g., high five) is made. The first team to hit all their tennis balls over the net wins.

Variations: 1. The location on the court from which to hit can change from baseline to service line to net in order to increase difficulty. 2. Hit forehand, backhand, or serve.

Players: 3-6 players per team in relay formation with 2 to 5 teams per court.

Equipment: Tennis balls, rackets.

Objectives:
1. Run fast and stop quickly.
2. Stroke ball across net with control.
3. Have fun.

66. Waiter and Waitress

Description: Players form lines on the baseline facing the net. Players on each team run, one at a time, with the tennis ball on their racquet around a marker (e.g., cone, racket, ball can) and back to their team before the other team. The team that completes the relay first with all players sitting in a line at the baseline wins.

Variations: 1. Carry more tennis balls on racket and in hand to increase the level of difficulty. 2. Add other obstacles. 3. Drape towel over non-racket arm. 4. Carry racket overhead. 5. Dribble ball on court or in air.

Players: 3-6 players per team in relay formation with 2 to 5 teams per court.

Equipment: Rackets, tennis balls, markers.

Objectives:
1. Develop wrist and arm strength.
2. Move quickly with racket control.

67. Zig Zag Tennis

Description: Players form two or three teams in relay formation behind baseline facing the net. Stacks of balls are placed at  baseline with a row of cones lined up toward net for each team. Players, in turn, put ball on their racket, Zig Zag through cones to net, and flip ball over net. Run back to baseline zig zagging through cones. First team to complete their shots and be seated at baseline wins.

Variations: 1. Use only one racket per team and pass racket. 2. Player who loses ball must start over. 3. Player who loses ball must fetch it and perform a tennis task (e.g., two-foot jump over racket handle 4 times) before continuing race. 4. Hit forehand, backhand, or serve when reach net. 5. Place tennis balls on the court.

Players: 3-6 players per team in relay formation with 2 to 5 teams per court.

Equipment: Tennis balls, rackets, cones.

Objectives:
1. Develop wrist and arm strength.
2. Balance.
3. Move quickly with racket control.

Summary

Tennis games in Munchkin II are games of low organization. They were selected for young children who are enrolled in their first or second series of tennis lessons. They are designed to acquaint Munchkins with the tennis ball, tennis racket, net, areas of the court, gripping the racket, forehand and backhand strokes, serving, hitting a bouncing ball, and hitting the ball off self-feeds.

Games in Munchkin II can be used as culminating experiences with the movement activities in the previous chapter. For more advanced Munchkins, lead-up games that resemble "real" tennis are presented in the next chapter.

CHAPTER 7

MUNCHKIN III
TENNIS LEAD-UP GAMES

This chapter, Munchkin III, includes games for children who are older, have more experience in tennis, or are just more skillful. It emphasizes lead-up games based on the concepts, strokes and rules of "real" tennis. This is the third chapter describing tennis activities and games.

Lead-up games allow more skillful children to advance their tennis game.

Lead-up games provide opportunities to use tennis skills in activities quite similar to tennis. They utilize forehand and backhand strokes, moving to the ball, playing with partners, team activities, and both a small and full-size court.

Munchkins find lead-up games fun and exciting. However, they also provide parents and astute players with feedback about the skills that need additional "work." For instance, some players hit too hard. They learn quickly in Tennis Baseball that hard hits are

outs. Controlled strokes count.

Games also provide built-in incentives for children. That is, young children will "work" on certain skills diligently when they know a favorite game will be played at the end of the lesson.

Tennis games

Lead-up games provide many opportunities to teach correct strokes, court position, effort, rules of play, and scoring. Winning and losing are clearly a part of these games. As a result, situations arise that help children understand the importance of following the rules, sportsmanship and etiquette.

In the activities and low organized games of the previous two chapters, parents could attend to as many as 30 children per court. Lead-up games are usually conducted with two to eight players per full court. This may require smaller groups or more parents depending on the availability of helpers and auxiliary teaching areas. Planning team play, player rotation, and the use of nearby teaching stations can maximize action and learning. Plan for maximum participation.

Certain games may not work well for all children. When this occurs, change the games in any way necessary to fit the skill level of your players.

69. Alley Rally

Description: Partners each place one ball on their alley line and take ready position 2-3 feet behind their ball. Game begins when one drop-hits ball attempting to hit opponent's tennis ball. Continuous rallying. Score one point by hitting opponent's ball. Play game to 1 or 2. Change partners frequently.

Variations: 1. Use only forehand or backhand. 2. Use one court, winners move up, losers move down. 3. Place one ball between players.

Players: Any number, 2-3 pairs per alley.

Equipment: Racket, tennis balls.

Objectives:
1. Hand-eye coordination.
2. Stroke with control, not power.
3. Move quickly while maintaining racket control.
4. Shift feet to get side to ball.

70. Around The World

Description: Players form two equal teams, one on each side of net in relay formation behind the service line. Play Munchkin Tennis using service courts. Players, in turn, hit the ball over the net into the opposite service court and go to the end of their line. Next Munchkin moves forward to play the return. Begin with a drop-hit serve. Players may not hit ace on serve. Team scores 1 point when opponent fails to return the ball. First team to 4 points wins.

Variations: 1. Use only one racket per team. 2. Eliminate players who do not make successful returns. 3. As singles game, players sprint to end of the line across net after their turn. Eliminate players as in Variation 2. Last two players "stay home" and conclude the game as a singles match. 4. For more advanced Munchkins, use the entire court with the most appropriate variation.

Players: Any number on two equal teams.

Equipment: Tennis rackets, tennis balls.

Objectives:
1. Watch the ball.
2. Learn to play tennis.
3. Court position and coverage.
4. Learn tennis scoring system.
5. Have fun.

71. Baseball Knockout Tennis

Description: Players line up in the alley with rackets and take turns batting as in baseball. Parent on the other side of the net throws or feeds the ball to each player at baseline. When players hit the ball in the designated areas, they are safe and can return to the dugout (alley) and await their next turn. When players miss, they must put their racket in the other alley and come to the side of the net with the parent. Player can rejoin the hitting side in the dugout by catching a ball. Start game with three or four players in designated area. The last remaining batter wins when all other players are in the designated areas trying to catch the ball.

Variations: 1. Batter's place on court can change from service line to baseline in order to increase difficulty. 2. Designate back-court, frontcourt or alleys as only areas for safe hits. 3. Hit forehand, backhand, or volley. 4. Ball may bounce one, two or three times before catching it depending on skill level of players. 5. Parent can deflect or pop up (with racket) hits so it can be caught more easily or direct ball away from fielders to protect batters.

Players: 6 to 12 players per court.

Equipment: Tennis balls, rackets.

Objectives:
1. Stroke ball with control, not power.
2. Develop hand-eye coordination.
3. Track ball in flight.
4. Move to the ball in order to catch it.

72. Beachball Volleyball

Description: Players are divided into two teams on each side of a 5' to 8' volleyball net, if possible. Players hit or punch beachball back and forth across net using as many hits as needed. Ball must cross the net when passing from one side to the other. Score as in tennis.

Variations: 1. Young children can catch and throw the ball as in the volleyball lead-up game called Newcomb. 2. Play Beachball Tennis at tennis net with children seated or kneeling.

Players: Two groups of 3 to 10 players.

Equipment: Beachball, volleyball net or rope with streamers.

Objectives:
1. Develop hand-eye coordination.
2. Track ball in flight.
3. Footwork.
4. Learn to play tennis.
5. Learn tennis scoring system

73. Blanket Tennis

Description: Players are in groups of 4 to 8 players with one small blanket per group. One or two groups on each side of net. Teams catch tennis ball in blanket and throw it back and forth across net as in tennis. To throw, start low then raise arms as the blanket is stretched tightly. Start match with toss from leader or from one team. Use tennis rules and scoring.

Variations: 1. Use larger volleyball or playground ball for younger children. 2. Ball may bounce more than once. 3. Use towels for younger players. 4. Use 6-8 players for large blankets. 5. See Towel Tennis on page 237.

Players: Groups of 4 to 8.

Equipment: Tennis ball, blankets or towels.

Objectives:
1. Teamwork.
2. Develop hand-eye coordination.
3. Track ball in flight.
4. Footwork.
5. Learn to play tennis.
6. Learn tennis scoring system.

74. Deck Tennis

Description: Singles. Toss deck tennis ring back and forth in upward flight release. Catch ring with one hand and immediately return ring with same hand. Begin play from behind right baseline with underhand forehand serve into opposite court. Alternate serving courts. Receiver catching the ring makes immediate underhand forehand return over net line into any part of opponent's court. Points awarded when miss, toss ring outside court (lines are in), catch with two hands, change ring to other hand after catch, hold ring too long, step over net line, and toss ring flat or downward. Score when serve. Play to 11, 15 or 21 points.

Doubles. Begin serve from behind right baseline. Opponents alternate receiving serve. Teammates serve in succession on side out. Any player may catch and make return after the serve.

Court dimensions: Like tennis court, 25' x 50' divided into four sections and service courts with net line in middle between each half.

Variations: 1. Use tennis scoring. 2. Play like Around The World on page 220.

Players: 2 or 4.

Equipment: Deck tennis ring, 7" diameter. Purchased or made from 2" tubing or stiff rope.

Objectives:
1. Develop hand-eye coordination.
2. Movement to the ring.
3. Speed, agility and rapid change of direction.
4. Court position and coverage.

75. Goodminton

Description: Bat softball or shuttle with paddle back and forth across volleyball net. Ball must be batted, not lifted or thrown. Three hits per side. Same person may not hit it twice in succession. Back line players may not spike in front of 10' line. Server has only one chance to clear net. Error results in side out. Volleyball scoring and rotation.

Court dimensions: 30' x 60' volleyball court with 8' net and 10' spiking line.

Variations: 1. Allow unlimited hits for younger players. 2. Use tennis scoring. 3. Adjust net height to suit players. 4. See Beachball Volleyball on page 222.

Players: Teams of 2-8 per side.

Equipment: Plastic or wooden paddles, tennis, sponge or badminton shuttle, volleyball net.

Objectives:
1. Develop hand-eye coordination.
2. Racket and ball control.
3. Court position and coverage.
4. Learn to play tennis.
5. Learn tennis scoring system.

Source: Saskatchewan Recreation and Fitness Division

76. Hand Tennis

Description: Partners hit ball back and forth across lines, alley, net, service court or backcourt. One hit per side. Use both hands. Ball must bounce across line, net or in alley. Play 1-4 point games in ladder format. Winner of each match moves up toward net and loser moves down alley for matches at baseline.

Variations: 1. Younger players catch and throw the ball. 2. Play on tennis court with players seated or kneeling. 3. Use larger balls. 4. Use wooden paddles to develop both hands. 5. Use coat hanger paddles and balloons.

Players: Singles, doubles.

Equipment: Tennis balls, wooden paddles.

Objectives:
1. Develop hand-eye coordination.
2. Track ball in flight.
3. Court position and coverage.
4. Learn to play tennis.
5. Learn tennis scoring system.

77. Head Of The Class

Description: Designate one court as top, Head of the Class. Bottom court at other end. Players use service courts for small court singles game. Two players per court. Play 1 point games using regular tennis rules. Player who wins the point moves up one court, loser moves down one court. Top and bottom players remain on same court. Shuffle order of players to start. Serve with drop-hit. Players may not hit ace on serve. Winner is player in top court after parent announces: This is the last match and it is for the Championship of the World and (your place). Also called King Of The Hill or Queen For A Day.

Variations: 1. Play 2, 3 or 4 point no-ad games when more time is available and skill level increases. 2. Play doubles matches in 1-4 point games on one entire court. 3. Play 2-3-4 per side in 1-4 point games on one entire court. Caution players about racket safety.

Players: 2-8 players per court.

Equipment: Tennis rackets, tennis balls.

Objectives:
1. Learn to play tennis.
2. Court position and coverage.
3. Learn tennis scoring system
4. Move quickly with racket control
5. Use strokes with accuracy.

78. Mini-Tennis

Description: Play ball over line, towel, bench, rope, chair, or net using single pair of service courts for singles matches. Play 4 point no-ad matches (i.e., 15-30-40-game) using regular tennis rules. Drop-hit to serve. Players may not hit ace on serve. Winner is first player to 4 points.

Variations: 1. Divide one tennis court from baseline to baseline with a rope or short nets. Use singles sideline as service line, baseline as end lines. 2. Play 2-3-4 players per side in 4 point no-ad games using service courts or entire court. Caution players about racket safety. 3. Play Head of the Class matches where players move up or down one court when win or lose.

Players: 4-16 players per court.

Equipment: Tennis rackets, tennis balls.

Objectives:
1. Learn to play tennis.
2. Court position and coverage.
3. Learn tennis scoring system.
4. Move quickly with racket control.
5. Use strokes with accuracy.

79. Munchkin Tennis

Description: Players use a single pair of service courts for a singles match, use both service courts for doubles matches. Play 4 point no-ad games (i.e., 15-30-40-game) using regular tennis rules. Drop-hit to serve. Players may not hit ace on serve. Winner is first player or team to 4 points.

Safety Note: Caution players about racket safety.

Variations: 1. Also called Little Tennis, Mini-Tennis, Short Tennis, and Tiny Tennis. 2. Play 2-3-4 players per side in 4 point no-ad games using service courts or entire court. 3. Play Head of the Class matches where players move up or down one court when win or lose. Winner is player in top court after parent announces: This is the last match and it is for the Championship of the World and (your place). 4. Play round robin, single or double elimination matches.

Players: 2-8 players per court.

Equipment: Tennis rackets, tennis balls.

Objectives:
1. Learn to play tennis.
2. Court position and coverage.
3. Learn tennis scoring system.
4. Move quickly with racket control.
5. Use strokes with accuracy.

80. One Wall Handball

Description: This game is similar to four wall handball and paddle ball. The 2' line on front wall is not used. Serve must bounce behind service line to start play. Ball may be played on one bounce or fly. Ball may not be caught. It must be hit with one hand, not two hands.

Court dimensions: 16' wide x 16' high 26' long with serving line 13' from wall. 2' line above floor on wall serves as net. Variations on this size are possible.

Variations: 1. Play with wooden hand paddles. 2. Score as in tennis. 3. Serve 5 points and change server. 4. Children can play Infinity Handball without fixed lines when the purpose of the game is to keep the ball in play.

Players: 2, 3 or 4.

Equipment: Tennis ball, sponge, rubber or handball, wall, tennis rackets or wooden paddles.

Objectives:
1. Learn to play tennis.
2. Court position and coverage.
3. Learn tennis scoring system.
4. Move quickly with control.
5. Use strokes from both sides of body with accuracy.

81. Paddle Ball (One wall)

Description: Singles. Players hit ball alternately against wall inside court markings and above 2' line on front wall. Server starts play by bouncing and hitting ball so it rebounds off wall inside court behind service line. Opponent must wait until serve bounces, then make return. Points are scored by server when opponent hits ball outside any court boundary, misses ball or fails to make good return on one bounce. Players may go outside court lines to play ball. Serve until miss or fault.

Doubles. Either teammate may play serve. After serve, teammates must play ball alternately. After first teammate loses the serve, partner serves.

Triples. Server plays against other two opponents (2 against 1) and alternates hits against either of the two opponents. Single player serves. Rotate to right backcourt when lose serve. Keep individual scores. Also called cut-throat.

Court dimensions: 16' wide x 16' high 26' long with serving line 13' from wall. 2' line above floor on wall serves as net.

Variations: 1. Score as in tennis. 2. First player to 11, 15 or 21 wins. 3. Serve 5 points and change server. 4. See Infinity Tennis.

Players: 2, 3 or 4.

Equipment: Wooden or plastic paddles, tennis rackets, tennis or sponge balls.

Objectives:
1. Learn to play tennis.
2. Court position and coverage.
3. Learn tennis scoring system.
4. Move quickly with racket control.
5. Use strokes with accuracy.

82. Paddle Tennis

Description: Singles. Hit ball back and forth across net on badminton size court. Begin play with serve from behind baseline by bouncing ball once and hitting it into opposite service court. Receiver must let ball bounce. After this, ball may be hit on fly or one bounce. Returns must bounce in either of the smaller front service courts. Play to 11, 15 or 21 points.

Doubles: Use the alleys. Alternate service courts. After the serve, either teammate may hit the ball. Serve and score as in tennis with server changing after each game.

Court dimensions: 18' wide x 39' long, 3' alleys, service line 10 1/2' from net with line down middle between service lines, 3' to 4' high net depending on skill level of players.

Variations: 1. Use tennis scoring. 2. Play like Around The World on page 220.

Players: 2, 3 or 4.

Equipment: Wooden or plastic paddles, tennis rackets, tennis or sponge balls.

Objectives:
1. Learn to play tennis.
2. Court position and coverage.
3. Learn tennis scoring system.
4. Move quickly with racket control.
5. Use strokes with accuracy.

83. Sidewalk Tennis

Description: Singles. Hit ball back and forth across center net line with either bare hand. Ball may be hit on fly or after one bounce. Serve from baseline by bouncing ball and hitting it over net line into court of opponent. Score only when serving. Change serve when lose. Play to 11, 15 or 21 points.

Doubles: Partners alternate serves, return of serve, and hits during each point.

Court dimensions: 6' wide x 24' long divided into 4 sections, 6' square. Net is center line. Base lines are between net line and rear lines. Can also use four sections of a sidewalk.

Variations: 1. Score as in tennis. 2. Place elevated rope across net line. 3. Use a larger ball for less skilled players. 4. Use wooden or plastic paddles.

Players: 2, 3 or 4.

Equipment: Tennis, sponge or rubber ball.

Objectives:
1. Learn to play tennis.
2. Court position and coverage.
3. Learn tennis scoring system.
4. Move quickly with control.
5. Use strokes with accuracy.

84. Solitary Tennis

Description: Single player with a tennis racket (wooden, plastic, racquetball, badminton, table tennis too) in each hand. Bounces a ball back and forth from one racket to the other. Count number of times able to bounce ball back and forth on each racket. Then partner tries.

Variations: 1. Bounce ball on court between each hit. 2. Partners with 4 rackets keep ball bouncing on ground or in air. 3. Construct 1' square paddle with net supported by nails and bounce table tennis ball back and forth across net.

Players: Single player or partners.

Equipment: Rackets, tennis balls.

Objectives:
1. Develop hand-eye coordination.
2. Racket and ball control.
3. Learn home practice activity.

85. Tennis Baseball

Description: Players form two even teams, one batters, the other fielders. Parent pitches (feeds) ball to batters in turn like baseball, anywhere from service line to baseline. Batters hit ball over the net. Ball landing in the backcourt is a home run, triple in alley, double in one service court and single in other service court. Fielders on opposite side of net attempt to catch each ball hit. Any ball caught on the fly or landing outside the court boundary is an out. Three strikes is an out; three outs and change sides.

Variations: 1. Alternate home run between alley and backcourt. 2. Move batters toward baseline to increase difficulty. 3. Hit ball to batter to increase difficulty. 4. Players hit forehand or backhand with or without warning.

Players: 3-6 players per team on 2 teams.

Equipment: One racket, tennis balls.

Objectives:
1. Watch the ball.
2. Hit the ball in a specific direction.
3. Hit ball with control, not power.
4. Track ball in flight.
5. Teamwork.
6. Have fun.

86. Tennis Volleyball

Description: Players form 2 equal teams on each side of net. Volley large beachball back and forth across net. Any number of hits per side with one or two hands or rackets are permitted. Ball must be hit upward. Use tennis serving and scoring system.

Safety Note: *Remind players about safety when rackets are used.*

Variations: 1. Adjust height of net, number of bounces, and one or two hand hits to the developmental level of players. 2. Must play ball in air before it bounces. 3. When played at tennis net, each hit that crosses the net must go upward.

Players: Any number on two teams.

Equipment: Tennis or volleyball net, large beachball.

Objectives:
1. Watch the ball.
2. Track ball in flight.
3. Develop hand-eye coordination.
4. Teamwork.
5. Have fun.

87. Towel Tennis

Description: Players are in 2-6 groups of 5 each with one racket, one large towel and 5 tennis balls. Of the players, 1 hits, 2 players hold towel and catch tennis balls, 1 feeds hitter, 1 retrieves misses. Hitter at baseline, catchers with towel in service court. Each player in turn hits one ball upward which is caught in towel on fly or bounce. Continue until each player hits one ball that is caught in towel. Take turns hitting, retrieving and catching until each player has a turn.

Variations: 1. Throw and catch a larger volleyball or playground ball for younger children. 2. Ball may bounce more than once. 3. Use 6-8 players for large blankets. 4. See Blanket Tennis on page 223.

Players: Groups of 5.

Equipment: Rackets, tennis balls, blankets or towels.

Objectives:
1. Develop hand-eye coordination.
2. Track ball in flight.
3. Teamwork.
4. Hit the ball in a specific direction.

88. Wall Rally Relay

Description: Players form team relay formation in front of an unobstructed wall without racket. One ball per team. On signal, first player in line tosses the ball against the wall, slides out of line and moves to the end of the line. Second player moves forward and catches ball, tosses ball against wall and goes to end of line. Repeat until all players have had 1-3 turns. Winner is first team to complete 1, 2 or 3 rounds without a miss.

Variations: 1. How many hits can your team make in time allotted before missing. 2. Start youngest players with large balls. Then use tennis balls. 3. Rally with hands. 4. Use tennis rackets with short strokes. 5. Use groundstrokes for more advanced players. 6. See Around The World on page 220, One Wall Handball on page 230, and Paddle Ball on page 232.

Players: 3-6 players on 2-4 teams per court.

Equipment: Rackets, tennis balls, wall space.

Objectives:
1. Develop hand-eye coordination.
2. Footwork.
3. Fast reaction to the ball, reflex action.
4. Evasive action to move away from the ball.
5. Speed, agility and rapid change of direction.

Summary

Tennis lead-up games are the third in a developmental progression or sequence of (1) tennis movements, ball and racket skills, followed by more advanced (2) low organized games. They were presented in Chapters 5 and 6. Lead-up games are used most successfully with young children who are familiar with the skills of tennis.

Lead-up games can be modified, made easier or more difficult, by changing the rules, limiting the strokes that can be used, or changing the number of players, objective or court size. Once children can play lead-up games like Munchkin Tennis successfully, they are nearly ready for "real" full-court tennis.

CHAPTER 8

MUNCHKIN IV
GRADUATED TENNIS METHOD

This chapter, for young beginners, is the last of four-consecutive chapters on tennis activities and games for children. It introduces the Graduated Tennis Method for Munchkins who have previous experiences in tennis.

The previous chapters, Munchkin I, II, and III, were devoted to tennis activities and games involving balls and rackets. Little attention was given to the skills and drills of tennis as they might be taught in group and private lessons.

This chapter describes the Graduated Tennis Method. In 1965, Dennis Van der Meer wrote a manual on learning tennis using a wooden paddle. His learning progression ended with a regulation racket. This program was used extensively by school districts and recreation departments throughout Northern California.

Some of the great tennis players of the world, including Pancho Gonzales, learned tennis using a graduated method.

Graduated Tennis Method or GTM, is a systematic learning method using modified rackets designed to facilitate such a program. The racket system is related not only to size, but to the skill of the student. Now, a number of GTM or junior rackets are commonly available in sporting goods stores, pro shops and discount houses. They are priced under $25.00.

Even though these rackets are designed for specific age groups, any beginning tennis player can learn quickly and easily starting with the smallest rackets. As students are able to execute the 10 steps outlined later in this chapter, they then "graduate" to the next size racket, assuming they are physically capable of handling it. It really makes no difference if the students are six or 16.

The size of the racket is in proportion to the size of the court.

The smallest racket should be used on a small court. It is defined by the service lines and the singles court sidelines. The net should be lowered to 27", the height of a standard racket. However, to begin GTM, the only equipment necessary is the palm of the hand and a tennis ball.

Graduated Tennis Method is a useful teaching method for three reasons:
1. Ease: It is easy to use.
2. Minimum frustration: Smaller rackets make the 10 steps easy and fast to learn.
3. Reward: Students are rewarded for skill development by graduating to the next larger racket.

The three points noted above plus smaller rackets and courts add up to a fast and effective way to learn. They make success more certain.

The key to Graduated Tennis Method is that learning is based on success, not frustration and failure. This is the secret of any successful teaching method.

The Graduated Tennis Method is a 10-step program.
1. The Grip, The Bounce.
2. The Rally Phase.
3. Playing Across The Net.
4. The Backhand.
5. Elementary Serve.
6. Advanced Serve (The Serving Rhythm).
7. The Forehand Volley.
8. The Backhand Volley.
9. Switching Grips.
10. Playing A Game And Scoring.

10 Step GTM Instruction

Step 1. The Grip, The Bounce.

A. The Forehand Grip. The correct grip is as easy as shaking hands. One partner holds the racket on edge and the other shakes hands with the handle. Repeat this many times being careful not to let the hand slip under the handle. Repeat until the grip feels comfortable.

Step 1 Activity: Shake Hands

Players form two circles, one inside and one outside, with players facing each other. Players circle slowly in opposite directions shaking hands with each person in turn.

B. The Rebound Off The Ground. Students keep the wrist firm, palm down, and bounce the ball off the ground with the hand. When they can do this 10 times in a row, repeat it using the racket. A firm wrist will help greatly. Practice until students can bounce the ball 10 times in a row with the racket.

C. The Rebound Off The Racket. Students turn the hand palm up and pop the ball up into the air. They practice this until it can be done 10 times with the palm of the hand. Repeat this using the racket with the correct grip.

Step 2. The Rally Phase.

A. Rebound Off Ground. Players stand about 4' from partners. Hit the ball gently with the hand and let it bounce on the ground toward the partner. Partners hit the ball back. When this is done 10 times with hands, it is repeated 10 times with rackets.

B. Learning To Judge Distance. Place two target balls 4' apart. Partners stand behind each ball. Use the same gentle hitting motion just practiced and hit partners' ball. After a few successful attempts, repeat the activity using rackets.

Step 3. Playing Across The Net.

A. Playing Across The Net. Lower nets to about 2' in the center. Place two target balls 4'-6' apart on either side of the net as in Step 2. Partners hit the ball over the net with hands aiming at the other ball. After 10 successful trials, repeat the activity using rackets.

B. The Rally. Remove the target balls and use hands to hit the ball back and forth over the net at least 10 times. Repeat this using rackets. Use very short strokes with almost no backswing.

Step 4. The Backhand.

A. The Grip. Children make a fist with thumb extended. Open the hand and place it on top of a racket handle with the thumb still extended. This is the basic backhand grip.

B. Strengthening The Backhand Grip. At first the backhand grip will feel weak but it will become stronger with practice. Using the backhand grip, students turn the back of the hand toward the sky (palm down) and bounce the ball until it can be done 10 times in a row.

C. Learning Depth. Repeat Rebound Off Ground (Step 2A) hitting backhands. Partners should make returns with backhands.

D. Judging Height And Distance. Repeat Step 3A with lowered net and target balls using backhands.

E. Backhand Rally. Repeat Step 3B rallying ball across a low net with partner using backhands.

Step 5. Elementary Serve.

A. Hand Phase. Youngsters stand sideways with feet comfortably apart. Place right hand (serving hand) behind the head, toss the ball up with other hand, and hit the ball with the palm of the hand. Repeat this 10 times.

B. Racket Phase. Youngsters hold the racket using the forehand grip. Place the racket behind the back. Toss a ball into the air and make contact with it as high as players can reach in the air. Start near the net so they will be successful immediately, then move away from the net one step at a time until behind the service line. Repeat this from the opposite service court until players hit 5, 10, 15 or 20 successful serves.

Step 6. Advanced Serve (The Serving Rhythm).

A. The Stance. Players stand sideways with feet comfortably apart. Hold racket in one hand and ball in the other, waist high. Start the racket down and swing up toward the back. At the same time reach toward the sky with the other (ball) hand.

B. Release And Catch. Repeat the same motion but release the ball and catch it in the extended hand.

C. Release And Hit. Repeat the preceding steps but hit the ball with the racket. Body weight shifts forward to the front foot. Racket makes contact with the ball as high as players can reach. When all of these parts are put together in a rhythmic movement, a smooth, powerful serve results. Practice this until players hit 5, 10, 15 or 20 successful serves.

Step 7. The Forehand Volley.

A. Hand Phase. Players stand like a policeman stopping traffic with palm of hand pointing toward partner. Toss ball to partner across the net who punches it back. Repeat this punch at least 10 times.

B. Racket Phase. Using a racket, players repeat Step 7A standing like a policeman stopping traffic with racket pointing toward partner. Hold racket with forehand grip. Toss ball to partner across the net and punch it back. Now keep the ball in play by letting the ball bounce on one side but not the other side. This is known as a forehand volley. Repeat this punch until it is played at least 10 times.

Step 8. The Backhand Volley.

Students take the same position at the net as in Step 7. Ask them to imagine they are going to punch the ball with their thumb. Hold racket using the backhand grip. Partners gently toss the ball at the racket. Hit it back with the same short punching motion used on the forehand volley. Repeat Step 7. Bounce the ball on one side and volley it on the other. Do this until partners play the ball 10 times.

Step 9. Switching Grips.

Players stand ready with a forehand grip. Partner hits ball gently and it is returned with a forehand shot. Quickly change to a backhand grip as partner prepares to return the ball to the backhand side. Alternate forehands and backhands. Practice until 10 alternate hits are successfully completed.

Step 10. Playing A Game And Scoring.

Partners stand 4'-6' apart. Using hands, no rackets, serve to partner and play a regular game. A clock face is drawn on the court substituting the points in tennis for the quarter hours: 15, 30, 40, game. Add in and add out can be learned later. Use the shortest racket and short court, lower the net if necessary, and play a game.

It is important that students, regardless of age, be able to play comfortably and successfully in the small court before attempting to play on the full size court.

Summary

The following skills are emphasized in the 10 Step Graduated Tennis Method. They are:
- Shake hands with the handle.
- Keep the wrist firm.
- Hit the ball gently with the hand.
- Use short strokes with almost no backswing.
- Alternate forehands and backhands.
- Punch the volley.

Skills emphasized in the serve are:
- Hold racket using forehand grip.
- Place the racket behind the back.
- Toss a ball into the air.
- Body weight shifts forward to front foot.
- Racket makes contact with ball as high as players can reach.
- Racket follow-through is down the side of front foot.
- Serve to partner and play a regular game.

The Graduated Tennis Method, Munchkin IV, is a way to introduce older and more capable beginners to the sport. Unlike the previous games and activities, GTM moves rapidly through the basic skills in a more direct manner. This method is well-suited to youngsters who have a broad activity background and serious-minded parents.

CHAPTER 9

PROGRAMS IN ACTION

This chapter describes a number of programs conducted for young children nine years of age and younger. It is included to provide more ideas for parents. These program ideas can be adopted completely or modified to fit your concept of how it could or should be done.

The material for this chapter was collected through telephone interviews conducted by Jack Hutslar, the author of Munchkin Tennis. Articles and other information were supplied by those who conduct the programs.

As the Munchkins' skills progress, the level of the programs can become more advanced.

Program examples are provided from cities around the United States, plus Holland and Sweden. Readers are referred to Gregg Presuto's program in this chapter beginning on page 253. It typifies the original philosophy and spirit of Munchkin Tennis.

If you are interested in starting a program or changing your own tennis program for young children, follow this suggestion. Read and study this chapter several times. It is full of great ideas. Once your own ideas start flowing, you will not be able to remember them all. Make notes about what you want to do. Then, find some courts and get moving.

Easy Tennis with Anneke Jelsma-de Jong
Uitgeest, Holland

Anneke Jelsma-de Jong, a tennis coach for 30 years and USPTR member, started Easy Tennis in Holland. She conducts it about 12 hours per week for students, beginning at age six or seven, in clubs and tennis halls.

In clubs, she limits enrollment to 16 students per session and introduces Easy Tennis to nearly 300 students yearly. A feature of Easy Tennis is that it can be taught and played indoors and outdoors, on all surfaces, in schools and in gymnasiums that are too small for regular tennis courts.

Racquetball rackets, soft touch balls and wooden hand paddles are used. Benches can serve as nets. Badminton courts make suitable Easy Tennis courts.

Easy Tennis is played on a small court. A tennis court is divided into four mini courts. Nets are strung from baseline to baseline at 80 centimeters, about 30 inches high, using the service court and singles or doubles sidelines. Matches consist of the best two out of three games to 15 points, winning by 2 points. Play begins with a bounce-underhand serve from behind the end line. Even score serves are taken from the right, odd scores from the left. Players change serves every 5 points and alternate servers starting each set.

Students are taught all strokes and they hit all the strokes. They include forehand, backhand, volley, lob, smash and the underhand serve. All strokes are done with a full swing. Children begin rallying 30 minutes after starting Easy Tennis.

The secret of Easy Tennis is small courts, racquetball rackets and light Tretorn ST (soft touch) tennis balls. She also uses a little ball machine. The combination of small court, small rackets and soft balls allows children to hit more balls in the same amount of time than they would on regulation courts. Children pick it up quickly.

According to de Jong, the basic principle of Easy Tennis is: It's easy to learn tennis when the ball is near the hand.

She believes the key to building a program for children is that it must be: (1) enjoyable, and (2) real tennis. Children know what tennis is through television. In Easy Tennis, children play all strokes. It is fun to learn, and they learn it quicker than real tennis. The better they can play, the more fun they have.

Children return to play two or three seasons, some up to age 11. It began with younger children in school but 13 to 14 year olds play it now. Even older people play enthusiastically.

The children really enjoy playing games of Easy Tennis using all the strokes. Easy Tennis tournaments are organized for them and that keeps interest high.

There was some difficulty early on with parents accepting Easy Tennis. They did not think Easy Tennis was real tennis. She began explaining to them in advance that the closer the hand is to the ball the easier it is for the children to play. They understood this and now accept the concept of Easy Tennis for their children.

At first some of the older children felt Easy Tennis was not real tennis. So in the beginning, she always encourages them, and asks them to try it. Once they try it, they become enthusiastic.

There are advantages to Easy Tennis. It is less expensive than real tennis and up to 16 children can play on one court. It is not difficult to get children involved. At clubs and in the schools, one child tells another.

Children of all ages like Easy Tennis, even older people. Make tennis easy in the beginning and they will learn the real game of tennis easier, because they will have a lot of experience hitting

every stroke. They are accustomed to the movements so it is easy to move up to the larger rackets and harder ball. de-Jong summed it up best when she said: "Easy Tennis is real fun and it is real tennis and that is what is important."

For more information about Easy Tennis, write: Anneke Jelsma-de Jong, Leeghwaterstraat 4, 1911 SB Uitgeest, Holland, or telephone 02513-11773.

Mini-Tennis with Leif Dahlgren
The Swedish Way

Leif Dahlgren is formerly the Development Administrator of the International Tennis Federation. He is a USPTR Master Pro and former director of Tennis Education in Sweden. He explained that Mini-tennis, the Swedish way, is how most children are introduced to tennis in that country. It is simply the game of tennis played on a dimensionally reduced court, a small court. Sponge balls are used because they travel slower and have less bounce than regular tennis balls. Beginners of all ages everywhere find this helpful. It gives players more time to react to the ball since many beginners do not move to the ball until it hits the court. Rebound activities can be conducted against walls or other surfaces when sponge balls are used. Both small and regular rackets can be used.

Smaller courts have no specific size requirements. Tennis courts can be divided into four smaller courts from baseline to baseline with short nets. Badminton courts work well but it can be set up on any surface, even lawns. Ropes between trees, benches or lines on the ground have also been used to form courts. Courts can accommodate from eight to 16 players at the same time. Singles and doubles play can take place at the same time.

Before long, young players can keep the ball going back and forth over the net. Soon they begin to develop game strategies, stamina, and a need to develop their tennis skills even more.

Since the ball is soft, players can take a full swing at the ball quickly. However, since the ball moves slower than regular tennis balls, players are more relaxed.

Mini-tennis, the Swedish Way, is competitive tennis right from the start, and it is fun. When they play mini-tennis and have fun the first few years, they continue to play and become more skillful. Playing, getting better and having fun is a natural process.

For more information, write: Leif Dahlgren, Liden 11B, 26931 Bastad, Sweden.

Munchkin Tennis with Gregg Presuto
Fox Chase Racquet Club
Chester, New Jersey

Gregg Presuto, USPTR National Tester at Fox Chase Racquet Club and sometimes summer instructor at the Van der Meer Tennis Center, conducts numerous tennis programs. Most of his participants are nine and under. His club offers a pro shop and four indoor courts open to the public.

They try to get six children in a group, one hour per week. A series of lessons may run eight to 10 weeks, meeting once a week. After-school programs can meet one to three times per week. Pros generally receive one-half of the fees generated.

The names and age groups used with his Munchkins are: Little Stars for ages 3-5, Rising Stars for ages 5-9 and Super Stars for older children ages 10 and up. Instructors may not have this much control over age groupings. Sometimes club management prefers to put ages 4 to 8 together in groups. As a rule, one and two year age groupings work best.

The best teaching situation is with six to eight children per court. Nevertheless, he has conducted Munchkin demonstrations in Singapore for 30 children without a court. On Hilton Head Island, South Carolina, Presuto has run summer resort Munchkin Tennis for groups of 6 to 30 children for the Van der Meer Tennis Center.

Gregg Presuto has been one of the
most innovative instructors for
Munchkin Tennis.

Additional teaching help is provided by assistant pros, parents and high school students. Equipment includes lots of tennis balls, hoppers, tubes and small rackets provided by the children.

This is how Presuto described Munchkin Tennis.

• Have a regular format or schedule to follow for all lessons. This helps children learn what to expect. Knowledgeable instructors also go on the court with a plan. Behavior improves when they know what is coming. They really look forward to their favorite games. He recommended that lessons take place twice per week. Good times are 4:00 P.M. and 5:30 P.M.

• He starts each lesson with warm-up exercises on the baseline. Children do arm circles, raise one foot and then the other in the air. While doing this with a new group, instructors can size up the children and see who will need help, or who is shy. Instructors can spot wild or cocky kids. They are usually the ones who are doing things faster than the others. This is a good time to learn names. It also gives children time to get things organized in their head. Warm-ups help break the ice. Children shuffle and do change of direction movements to a whistle. This causes them to bump together and laugh. Laughter is a signal that everything is OK and it is time to get rackets.

• Racket and ball exercises occur next. Children learn exercises they can do at home when it is raining. Some are ball sense exercises, like Ups and Downs, they can practice anywhere. Munchkins are asked to bounce the ball up to 10 times, then down, alternate sides and then sides and frame. Change frequently to make it more exciting. Challenge the better players by asking them to do more difficult things. Ask the more skilled to dribble it like a basketball.

• After the racket and ball activities, start the volley. It is an easy stroke for them and instructors can do the most with it.

• Then cover the serve. This gives them a chance to rest after more vigorous activities.

• Then do groundstrokes.

• Finish with the overhead.

• A different stroke can be done each week, or each day in a daily program.

• The last day, Presuto does "The Best of Carson." Children pick their favorite games and relays. He said that it has been very successful at his club.

Presuto offered a few other suggestions.

• Do activities the children find easy and move through them quickly.

• The one-hand forehand and two-hand backhand are taught to ages 5-6, but he said: "We do not mess with the grips too much. When they get to ages 7-8, I show them the backhand grip. Put the thumb behind handle for a better backhand."

• When a child falls on the court, he does not run over to them. He watches them. They usually get up and join back in without problems. He does not mother them when they fall.

• Some children improve fast. After a while when the children get better, you have to move them up to keep the program going. Presuto suggested that instructors form separate groups of more skilled children, but numbers are needed to make it work. That is, groups of six to eight skilled players are needed. This may not be feasible in smaller programs.

• Misbehavior can be treated humorously. For instance, when children misbehave, he stuffs tennis balls in his shirt to look like muscles. Then they are cautioned about being on their best behavior.

• For children who appear to be hyperactive, Presuto asks them to sign a contract that they will not eat candy or drink colas (caffeine) before each lesson. This helps them control themselves.

Despite Presuto's assortment of activities and games, he described his version of Munchkin Tennis as having no set format. That is, he knows what he plans to do each lesson before going on the court, but he is flexible. He uses many different games, and can pick and choose from them instantly depending on the physical characteristics, interests and skill level of a particular group. Presuto collected or developed and graciously provided many of the games included in Chapters 5 and 6 of The USPTR Manual of Munchkin Tennis.

Presuto's Munchkins enjoy relay games the most. Older Munchkins enjoy Tennis Baseball, as others have reported. Younger ones like Golf Tennis (called Coconut Tennis in New Zealand), Sandwich Tennis and Dizzy Lizzy. Like most teachers, Presuto agrees that children love to compete in races as long as the atmosphere remains fun.

Presuto would not say that his fun-oriented activities and games approach to tennis is unique because he does not know what other instructors do. However, some of the relay games like Triple Decker Sandwich are different. He said: "I will take as many kids as are there and make one big sandwich with all the Munchkins as a team. You must put the strongest children on the bottom for it to work."

He has conducted some special events. For instance, instructors wear bunny ears at Easter or dress up in green on St. Patrick's, pilgrims at Thanksgiving and Santa at Christmas. At the Van der Meer Tennis Center resort, a staff member dresses up as Uncle Sam each 4th of July.

Presuto said that he has few problems with parents. He gives them an outline before lessons begin and tells them what will be covered. He emphasizes fun and an introduction to tennis, not technical stroke production. When parents feel this is not enough, he tries to arrange semi-private lessons for them with another child. Presuto talked about his motives when he said: "I want to keep it fun so when they get bigger, they will want to stay with tennis."

The club's Munchkin program is advertised through printed brochures. They are available to anyone who comes into the pro shop. He believes that instructors overlook a large source of revenue when they ignore the nine and under age group. Instructors may not realize that many future lessons will come from Munchkins when they get older and better. There are fewer advanced players than Munchkins and many of them just want to hit so they are not a great source of revenue for lessons.

At resorts, where people may come just for a week, the Munchkin program runs daily, Monday through Friday for two hours per day. Young children play Munchkin Tennis giving parents free time to engage in other vacation activities. It is an attractive selling point for parents when they know there are well organized events for their children.

Regarding mistakes, Presuto offered these helpful comments. He injects humor into the classes but he tries not to be too funny. Instructors need to learn how much is the right amount of humor. If you do it too much, it takes longer to regain control of the group. Examples of humor include:

- Groan when hit by a ball.
- Let a ball bounce off your head or take a spill when a ball hits you in the head.

- Drag out the start of relay races with a sneeze, rather than say "go". This produces false starts which children always enjoy.
- Carry balls on the racket and "steal" a ball from someone. Presuto has learned how to punch their racket down and slide his racket down and under to catch their tennis balls on his racket.
- A "magic trick" that impresses young children is to throw a ball high in the air and catch it on the racket. Most instructors can learn this trick with practice. Learning to stop a flat drive takes a bit more practice.
- When there are not enough ball hoppers, children will stuff balls in their shirts and instructors can make comments about how much weight they have gained.
- Do high fives for good shots, and act like it hurts your hand.

Presuto summarized his feeling about working with Munchkins this way. "The kids are enjoyable. I feel energized after my classes with them. It is funny. I never thought I could like anything more than winning a match or tournaments but the feeling after working with kids comes close."

For more information, write: Gregg Presuto, 138-B Black River Road, Long Valley NJ 07853, or telephone 908-879-5231.

Munchkin Tennis with Teresa Phillips
Joe White Tennis Center
Winston-Salem, North Carolina

Teresa Phillips is a high school math teacher and tennis coach who teaches Munchkin Tennis on city courts using junior rackets and regular tennis balls. This program, started in 1986, is conducted for three to six year olds each summer. They meet for three weeks, twice per week in 30 minute sessions. Cost is approximately

$30 per student and Munchkin Tennis must pay for itself.

This program evolved when five and six year olds began showing up for lessons with the older seven to 18 age groups. The little ones had to be treated differently. It helped also that parents asked for a separate program for younger ages.

Now, Munchkin Tennis involves anywhere from three to 22 children. Most of the time, three courts are used with a student-teacher ratio of 4 to 1, 4 children per court. Usually, five classes are run during the year with an average of 40 students per season. It has stayed about the same size each year, with a lot of repeats.

Children are placed on three courts by age. The older ones hit tennis balls and move to hit the first day. In comparison, three-year olds must have everything done right for them. That is, they are more successful when instructors put the ball where they are swinging.

Assistance with the program is provided by high school juniors and seniors or college students. Many play tennis, have helped before, or grew up in Young Folks Tennis and began helping with Munchkin Tennis. Young Folks Tennis is sponsored by Winston-Salem Tennis and the City Recreation Department. It is free for children, ages seven to 18.

Munchkin Tennis follows this format:

Lesson One. Introduction. Do not hit the ball. Work on hand-eye coordination, ball toss, stepping to hit a ball, catching the ball, relay events with rackets, balance ball on racket and walk to designated spots.

Lesson Two. Children may begin hitting balls. Work on forehand side, not over net, just to make contact. When skill level of players is higher, begin hitting ball over the net.

Lesson Three. Work on backhand side. Children usually have more success with two hands, more stability.

Lesson Four. Continue to practice forehand and backhand. Play games where they get balls over the net, and receive a prize or reward.

Lesson Five. Work on forehand volleys, then backhand volleys.

Lesson Six. Put it all together. Do some of each, play games, see how many balls you can get over the net or to a certain place. Do relay races between hitting.

Phillips noted: "We try to make it fun for them, but we feel this is true for any program. Some of our relay races may not be related to hitting a tennis ball, they are just fun. We work for a good mix of what we want them to learn and what they think is fun."

Activities the children enjoy vary from class to class. Some groups just like to hit the ball over the net. This past summer they liked picking up tennis balls. It was turned into a contest to see how many balls could be stacked on a racket.

Concerning problems, Phillips said that the biggest mistake we made initially was keeping them in groups that covered a wide age span. It was difficult to keep the attention of younger players.

Phillips, in speaking about problems, said: "Parents are very supportive. For instance, if they see a behavior problem with their child, they will back you up."

She continued: "We were afraid to take care of behavior problems for fear parents would be upset. This turned out to be less of a problem than we expected. However, in club situations, this may be a problem. I suggest that instructors speak with a parent before doing anything."

Advertising the program started with television interviews on the news. This resulted in many telephone calls and children enrolled. Since then, word of the program has spread by word of mouth. It is advertised only in a booklet published by the park and a listing in the calendar section of the daily newspaper.

In summary, Phillips said: "I think Munchkin Tennis is a good program because it gives children the opportunity at an early age to see what the game is like. It gives them a foundation if they want to continue. Our oldest ones are eight now."

For more information, write: Teresa Phillips, 1134 Century Park Avenue, Kernersville NC 27284, or telephone 919 993-6910.

Pee Wee Tennis with Colleen Cosgrove
Net Tennis
Princeton, New Jersey

Colleen Cosgrove, a physical education graduate and U.S.P.T.R certified tennis pro, was formerly Executive Director for Princeton Community Tennis Program in Princeton, New Jersey. It is a non-profit tennis organization using or renting six different facilities including two indoor centers, plus university, township and high school courts.

Among their programs is Pee Wee Tennis for four to six year olds, and a junior elementary program for 2nd to 4th graders and 3rd to 6th graders. There is another program for 4th graders and up. When necessary, Pee Wees are divided into skill levels within classes. When outstanding progress occurs, separate classes of intermediate Pee Wees lasting 60 minutes are set up so they can play with others of similar skill levels.

The program runs four seasons and serves over 600 children. There are eight week Spring and Fall seasons, an eight to 10 week Summer program, and two 12-week indoor seasons, October through March. Pee Wee classes meet for 30 minutes once a week. They also offer sessions meeting two and three times per week. More advanced and intermediate Pee Wees meet for 60 minutes weekly. The seven to 18-year olds have 90 minute sessions.

Cost of the program to students ranges from $20 to $55 per session, depending on the length and whether they meet at indoor or outdoor courts. However, they offer scholarships to needy students so no child is ever turned away for lack of money.

The student-teacher ratio is 4 to 1 on the average with a maximum of 12 students in a class. Helpers consist of at least two qualified instructors and one high school assistant for each class. Cosgrove trains a summer staff of 50.

She has used short nets with her Pee Wee Tennis since 1981. Most Pee Wee Tennis is done on one to three tennis courts with short nets and a wall or backboard. Short rackets are sold to students.

The equipment used includes: sponge balls, fleece balls, Tretorn slow bounce balls, cones, balloons, and hula hoops. Tennis Target Trainers and Poly Spots are used as targets and markers for obstacle runs. Much of her equipment was ordered through the USTA and some through the USPTR.

Cosgrove likes to make holiday theme targets from construction paper. Pumpkins, pilgrims, Easter bunnies, and Santa provide good court or wall targets for hitting games.

The emphasis of the program is fun, not to develop champions. The curriculum plan emphasizes introductory stroke work, ball and racket readiness drills, tracking skills, eye-hand coordination, listening skills, learning to share and act cooperatively, and meeting new friends.

Pee Wees work on ups and downs, volley, forehand, backhand, from service line, a modified overhead, serving from net and service line, and combinations like forehand and volley. The four-year olds will even do split steps in volleying. Pee Wees also play mini doubles, rally, play baby mini-tennis against the wall, and learn to keep score.

The 2nd to 4th graders do more stroke work, volley, play short tennis, learn a modified serve, and keep score. They play many little fun group games.

Cosgrove does skill tests with children beyond the Pee Wee level. They receive badges and stars. They will go home and practice their ups and downs until they can do 100. It provides a good measure of their ability and how well the staff is doing. Kids see their improvement.

A favorite activity of the Pee Wees is running. Cosgrove said: "Pee Wees just love to run and be active. Most older kids would feel like we are working on conditioning if we did the running games with them that we do with the Pee Wees. In fact, Pee Wees would rather run around 10 times than once. You can see how easily they knock over cones and cans during games. Running really helps develop their kinesthetic awareness."

They conduct special events around the holidays, give free clinics and a tennis carnival for the county. In class, they can win posters, hats, and other holiday candies by hitting targets. She gives candy corn at Thanksgiving, bunnies at Easter and candy canes at Christmas. She would prefer to give health food but it is too expensive. Cosgrove also tries to make activities educational. That is, children can earn letters that spells Pilgrim or Turkey in a game, rather than points.

The Princeton Community Tennis Program is advertised with printed brochures. They are sent bulk mail to 14,000 Princeton residents, and 4,000 non-resident participants on the mailing list. Extra copies are placed in local sporting goods stores and tennis centers. They also offer free school clinics and free junior clinics.

Regarding mistakes she has made that others might avoid, she said: "I think I teach too much one handedness. I would like to spend more time developing both sides of their body as is needed in basketball and soccer. It would be good to make them more two handed and two sided. This could be done by adding more ball skills without the racket. However, when we have only 30 minutes per week and have to pay court time, it is difficult to justify activities that are not pure tennis racket and ball oriented."

Cosgrove also emphasized the need for activity or action in the program. She said: "If you do not keep it moving, you lose them."

She disagreed with some experts who recommend a variety of non-tennis activities for young tennis players. She believed children must have experiences related to real tennis. To make her point, in an extreme case, she told of one little girl from a tennis family who stopped attending after only two lessons. Cosgrove found out later the girl wanted the ball hit to her off the racket, not tossed. Tossing was not tennis to her.

Cosgrove believes key things are helpful in starting programs for the nine and unders. They include:
• offer free first-time lessons so children can try tennis without feeling financially committed to a program when the child is tentative about doing new things. Be flexible with first-time players.
• group children by ability.

Regarding ability grouping she said: "We still mix them up in Davis Cup format team games. Number one players from each team play each other all the way down to number sixes. When we put them on teams together, it helps in learning names, sportsmanship and spirit. They help each other."

Cosgrove's attitude toward Pee Wee Tennis is obvious. She said: "We are not out to teach them topspin backhands crosscourt. In fact, we encourage them to play a lot of sports. We do not make them come if they do not want to come. We want the children to want to come to tennis."

For more information, write: Colleen Cosgrove, 77 Herrontown Lane, Princeton, NJ 08540, or telephone 609-921-1864.

Preschool Tennis with Marceil Whitney
Redmond, Washington

Marceil Whitney is a tennis professional at several centers in Redmond and has been teaching and coaching tennis for 17 years. She has worked with tennis players as young as age three, through adults. Whitney developed a tennis program for preschool children.

Whitney has been teaching little ones for 10 years. Her system evolved through trial and error and success. She said: "I learned to be very flexible and grow. I start looking for new ideas when I feel I am getting in a rut."

The program, which does not have an official name at this time, is grouped for children ages 3-4, 5-6, 7-9, and 4-6. She normally uses one court with six children, and up to eight per court with the 7-9 year olds.

The 3-4 and 5-6 year olds were called Court Jesters, and the 4-6 year olds were called Super Mites. The 4-6 year old grouping is for children who are a bit more advanced. The 7-9 year olds were called the Hits and Giggles.

The preschool program is offered through the local parks department and private clubs. Both indoor and outdoor courts are available. It costs approximately $11 for four 30-minute sessions, twice per week in summer and once per week in fall. At the club, the cost is approximately $39 for 6 hours, in 30-minute sessions.

About 300 preschoolers were enrolled in a recent eight-month season. The ratio of boys to girls is about the same and it has been done with parents and children together. For the most part, she teaches by herself, although her oldest son has helped periodically.

Whitney works with a lot of eye-hand coordination in a fun and positive way, with the emphasis on fun. There is very little stroke analyzing or stroke perfection. Confidence and self-esteem are emphasized so they can work on other things in life. Children progress according to their ability, not her expectations or parents.

Some of the equipment used includes balloons, stringless rackets or frames and visual aids that relate to tennis. Preschoolers progress from balloons to beach balls to playground balls to nerf balls and then tennis balls. It is done in progressive steps so they will be successful when they get to tennis balls.

Games include fun things that keep them moving. There is very little standing around which also keeps their attention. For instance, they are timed as they run around the net to pick up balls. It keeps them busy learning skills. Running is good for footwork. Picking up balls reminds them to bend their knees.

Among the favorite activities are hitting tennis balls, games, and Tennis Baseball. There are no tournaments. A special event they enjoy is the Halloween Party. Pumpkins are placed on the court and they try to hit them.

The underlying philosophy of Whitney's program was stated clearly when she commented: "My main objective is to give them a fun thing to do and learn tennis. Fun is the main objective. If this is fun, they will carry it out the rest of their lives."

She felt she was doing it correctly, that is, keeping it fun. She offered evidence in that she has taught children as young as two and one-half years of age. Some children are now seven and eight and have come back three and four years. She was particularly proud of a seven-year old who can play games on the service court. Whitney said: "If they like it and keep coming back, they will become little tennis players."

A feature of Whitney's program is unique in these ways. She said: "When I work with three-year olds, I treat them more like my own child. They need reassurances that they are important. Sometimes they feel they are not as important as their older brothers and sisters who play tennis and other sports. Playing tennis gives them a feeling of importance so they can compare themselves more favorably to their brothers and sisters."

She continued: "It is OK for them to talk with me. I do a lot of bonding where I become friends or companions with them, rather than establish the traditional teacher-student relationship. I also keep everything very light, no pressure."

She suggested that teachers who are not familiar with children should observe others who teach youngsters and see how they operate. Go to preschools and see what they do. Watch other sports in this age group. Ask questions of other pros with programs. Watch Sesame Street. She has incorporated much from that program into tennis.

Whitney won the USTA Seminar Contest and helped market the concept nationally as will a book about the program and eventual video. The book provides teaching aids, lesson plans and marketing information about the program.

Expansion involves advertising. Whitney has collected comments from parents. She said they have written things like: "We continue to come back because our kids love it. They are having fun, and I do not care if they learn tennis. Their self-esteem has improved so much as a result of tennis." Whitney is proud, as any person might be, that she has developed a clientele that follows her to where she teaches.

Whitney cautions teachers about the crying child: "Do not make them come on the court. Go back periodically and check to see that they are still there. Then, encourage parents to come out on the court with the child. Do not insist on them doing something they do not want to do or cannot do. Be patient and flexible and let them do it when they are ready."

Whitney believes you must build friendships so they will want to come onto the courts. At first, fearful children really bothered her, but she has learned to handle it now.

Regarding mistakes she has made, she noted that classes for the Parks Department have been very successful. There have been as many as 18 on the waiting list. However, she qualified this by saying: "I tried to accommodate those waiting and add more classes. This drained me mentally because you must constantly be on top of things with the little ones. I did better when I limited the number of classes. I love doing what I do so it is easy for me to say yes, but I must limit the number of hours I teach this age group."

Whitney found it helpful to start with three-year olds and move up the age group ladder through the day, rather than down the ladder or skip around. She noted that it may not work that way for other people.

Whitney summed up her feelings with these thoughts: "Working with this age group is a way to let the kid out in yourself. You can be a kid too, and they love it when you can be one of them. You stay young working with little ones. It puts a whole new perspective on life. It is rejuvenating."

For more information, write: Marceil Whitney, 16219 NE 95th Court, Redmond WA 98052, or telephone 206-881-1446.

Tennis Buddies with Jim Brown
American Youth Tennis Foundation
El Toro, California

"Tennis players need to have the skills of a switch hitter in baseball, have the mind of a football quarterback, the defensive skills of a basketball player, the footwork of a soccer player, and the control of a golfer." This is how Jim Brown, the founder of Tennis Buddies, describes good tennis players.

Brown worked with young children and saw how expensive tennis was for them. He wanted to get more kids involved, so he got a few people behind him whose sons were taking lessons with him. A couple of men put up $25,000 to give free tennis classes in 13 cities in 4 counties. They used two vans, and purchased seven ball machines. They took 190 kids at a time and it received a big response.

Unfortunately, the kids had no tennis to turn to when they left in their vans. This led to developing a tennis system where the kids played and parents became involved.

Then they saw that the kids did not want to just hit balls, they wanted to play games. Wanting to make the instruction fun, they developed a target game called "Skills" which leads to match play. It evolved into an instructional league with teams of 4-5 to learn strokes.

Youngsters spend 45 minutes on strokes and 45 minutes in games. By the next session, they have a scoreboard with standings, and the kids and their parents get excited about learning new shots.

A progression was developed including a system whereby players graduate into a varsity program. The original motive in Brown's system was to find talent and develop it for tournament tennis. Several ranked players and others with national championships came out of it.

However, in researching what they were doing, Brown found that his kids did not have much fun. This was not how they wanted the kids to feel. Then they devised a new system and Brown's children, who are now 14, 11 and 2 years of age, went through it.

Now, they have started over 60,000 people in 11 years. Brown's young tennis players have won over 50 tournaments, and over 100 of the 17 USTA section tournaments. It is the largest independent tennis program ever developed in the USA. To make it self-sustaining, he offered it to tennis instructors.

Tennis Buddies is team oriented. This gives them something in common with other children in neighborhood. They will get together and go play tennis.

Now, it is targeted toward developing high school teams and sold as preventive medicine for young children. This way, Brown is able to keep the family involved. All families did not stay involved when he emphasized the national tournament system. It required more individual family initiative.

This became the National Instructional Starters League or Tennis Buddies. It was done throughout Southern California then taken nationally in 1984. They kept local control until they knew how it would all work.

It began with volunteer parents and was structured like youth soccer and baseball, but less costly. Instruction always came up as a need in tennis compared to soccer and baseball. Yet, parents felt uncomfortable because they did not know the sport. When parents left, a void appeared again. Brown solved this snag in the program by franchising Tennis Buddies to local tennis instructors.

Children are provided with uniform shirts for their team. There is a lot of rooting for each other. Hooting, hollering and having fun. Brown suggested that parents keep score, help pick up balls and keep the activity going.

For the tennis parent or instructor, Tennis Buddies features Income, Instruction, and Progression based on points scored. The key is a pro who directs the program and markets himself to the community. It will put tennis teachers in touch with 400 families a year.

National sponsors such as adidas were recruited. They became involved because Brown collected the following kind of data:

- 80% of the children immediately purchase junior rackets and shoes.
- 59% of the children sign up for another session.
- 67% of the returning participants purchase equipment within the year.
- 29% of the parents pick up the game themselves, buy equipment and make it a part of their lives.

Instructors are able to get a good number of youngsters involved in this system. They can start 256 players in three, nine week programs a year. It can develop into a year-round varsity program for the high school. Players are developed, there is no pressure and it is inexpensive.

Tennis Buddies features six to 10 players per court. Attention span is always a concern when dealing with children under the second grade. In Tennis Buddies, they only need it for 5-10 minutes because there is constant change. Children are constantly moving.

Players are named the Junior Future Stars or Future Stars. Those age nine and over are called Match Play Preps. They separate players at age eight feeling that most of the nine year olds are strong enough to hit from the baseline.

The five- and six-year old Junior Future Stars play from service line to the service line. Their target is inside the service line and they hit straight ahead.

The seven- and eight-year old Future Stars play from the service line to the baseline. Their targets are in the backcourt and they start serving.

The Match Play Preps for ages nine and over hit down the line and crosscourt. Shots in the alleys do not count as much. In the team system of Tennis Buddies, matches are usually close.

Next, players move into the varsity training program. Some of these youngsters are as young as seven years old when they have passed through the system.

Children are motivated to do well because a lot of rewards are provided through a token economy. They receive certificates and prizes according to points scored. They receive tickets for being on time, for answering questions, and for scoring in the 5's and 10's competition. Players receive more rewards each week in Tennis Buddies than in the other sports.

The daily format is: be on time, go to the court, instruction, do the first stroke, answer questions, receive tickets, instruction, work on second stroke, answer questions, receive tickets, combine both strokes, do the 5s and 10s competition, and receive tickets. It also includes raffles, skills match with 1-2-3-4 on one team against 1-2-

3-4 on other team. They rotate in and out and standings are kept for teams and individuals with more tickets awarded. Prize raffles are held for players and parents who help.

If the children get wild, their tickets are taken away and they are given back at raffle time, if they behave. Parents watch and see that it is totally organized.

Brown said that it took a long time to develop the court. It is easy to set up and uses plastic molds, ropes and blocks that extend two feet beyond the baseline.

Special events that create interest are tournaments, city against city. All three skill divisions compete and everybody sends players for each age group.

Concerning mistakes Brown made along the way, he said: "I was very competitive, and I wanted a program that would develop national champions. I was that type of person, but our best players were not having fun playing in that system. Taking away the childhood of those kids is the worst thing you can do."

"We saw too much nasty stuff in the tournament system: parents and kids making obscene gestures, and parents hitting other parents over the head with chairs. In one tournament, a young player had 19 overrules because winning was the most important thing to him. My ego was being served, not the kids. Now, I have gone to the exact opposite."

"We are getting kids who love the game now. Parents want to develop a child with whom they can play tennis. That is the beauty of it. You have a partner right in the house. Now we see former players coming back with their kids."

For more information, write: Jim Brown, American Youth Tennis Foundation, 20331 Lake Forest Drive, Suite C-11, El Toro CA 92630, or telephone 714-454-8577.

Tiny Tennis with Jack Hutslar
Sedge Garden Swim and Racquet Club
Kernersville, North Carolina

Jack Hutslar managed a small 225 family member swim and racket club that featured three lighted outdoor tennis courts. Group tennis lessons were offered in June, July and August. The cost of lessons was $12 for eight-one hour sessions meeting three days per week. Other instructional programs include a Spring and late Summer 15 hour tennis school and two month Spring and Fall instructional league for experienced players.

Most of the group lessons at the Sedge Garden Swim and Racquet Club in Kernersville, North Carolina were taken by children age 12 and under. Lessons were divided into teens, 10 to 12's, and nine and under Tiny Tennis. The club is in a suburban location. Children were driven to and from lessons by parents, mostly mothers.

Lessons began with a brief explanation to parents about objectives. Parents were asked to purchase a junior racket and three new tennis balls for their children. They were encouraged to come to the courts at other times and play with their children.

Hutslar began Tiny Tennis with movement education activities featuring a variety of balls. Youngsters learned to bounce, dribble, toss, throw and catch tennis balls. He found that young children who grew up in non-sporting families had not developed hand-eye coordination. Therefore, as much as one-third of the time in the first four lessons was devoted to fun-oriented ball handling activities. He used tennis balls, junior basketballs, sponge balls, soccer balls and even footballs. Children were asked to try different movements with their ball. They exchanged balls frequently learning that not all balls are alike. These movement activities were described in Chapter 5.

Among their favorite activities were dribbling, tossing the ball in the air, turning 360 degrees and catching it, and throwing and catching across the net. The latter provided an early introduction to serving. They even started learning to juggle tennis balls.

Players learned to control the racket and ball by bouncing balls up and down off both racket faces. Ups and downs and partner bumps were a part of each lesson.

Follow The Leader was a popular early activity where many tennis skills were used. Children followed the lines of the court, go over and around the net bouncing the ball many ways. It was also used to locate, identify, and name parts of the court.

The one hand continental and two hand backhand grips were taught. Stroke instruction, which was a part of each lesson, began as the instructor dropped balls at the service line. Children attempted to hit balls into the backcourt.

As they improved, Hutslar tossed the ball from beyond the net, from the opposite service line, and from the baseline. Youngsters gradually moved back to the baseline. Finally, balls were hit to players from the baseline, baseline to baseline, just keeping the ball in play.

Children take more interest in rallying under two circumstances. First, when children are able to hit the ball over the net, it is returned for them to hit again. They can stay in as long as they continue to hit the ball. Second, teams of 3-5 players keep score of the number of times their teammates are able to hit the ball over the net into the singles court or into the back court.

Other popular games that helped children learn tennis and have fun at the same time were Alley Rally, Beachball Volleyball, Tennis Baseball and Tiny Tennis.

Tennis Baseball helped over-eager children learn to hit the ball with control. In this game, the court is divided into areas for a single, double, triple, and home run. Anything landing outside the court is an out. It can be played 3-6 per side.

The game of Tiny Tennis resembles regulation tennis. It is played in either one or two service courts as singles or doubles. Players can hit the ball on one or two bounces but service aces are not permitted. They begin by playing one-point matches in either round robin or ladder formats as in Head Of The Class. When they became more skillful, they played Around The World using Tiny Tennis courts.

During lessons, children received brief chalk talks during shade breaks. They include sportsmanship and manners, Say No To DAT (drugs, alcohol and tobacco), diet and nutrition, fitness, concentration and doing well in school.

At the conclusion of eight lessons, young children were surprisingly skillful. Hutslar conducts a little award ceremony for them on the last day. They receive a certificate with their name on it and a trophy with their name on it. The trophy is actually a banana inscribed with their name and MVP, Most Valuable Person.

They must peel and eat their banana immediately. They are told that trophies symbolize they have accomplished something. However, some people stop trying to improve once they receive "their" trophy. By eating their trophy, youngsters are reminded there is more to learn, and if they continue to play tennis and try hard, they will improve.

The point is, and it applies to all of us, we cannot sit back once we have accomplished something. We must keep striving, particularly aspiring athletes and sport entrepreneurs.

For more information, write: Jack Hutslar, North American Youth Sport Institute, 4985 Oak Garden Drive, Kernersville NC 27284, or telephone 919 784-4926.

Summary

The tennis programs for young children described in this chapter are dynamic. Activities change from week to week and season to season depending on the characteristics of those who enrolled. Each time these stories are read and studied, new ideas will come to your mind.

Regardless of how these people conduct their tennis for young children, they have four things in common. (1) Most come face-to-face with 300 or more young tennis players each season. (2) They do what they do because they enjoy children. (3) Parents know the objectives of their programs, understand the purposes of the activities and are satisfied and supportive. (4) Fun is the overriding objective of their respective programs. When the children have fun, they return to play again and again.

CHAPTER 10

HOW TO START MUNCHKIN TENNIS

Starting your own tennis program is an exciting challenge. The following items should be put on the agenda for careful consideration when starting Munchkin Tennis. They will help you conduct successful programs. They are: children, staff, a facility, a plan, equipment, ways to tell others of the program, and parents. This chapter concludes with a bibliography, sources of information for working with young children, and a summary.

Children

The first requirement for Munchkin Tennis is children. This is not a problem when children live near tennis facilities. Yet, it is important to know or find out the characteristics of the local population. Call it demographics. When tennis is not a highly visible sport in your community, you will have to start from ground zero and build. This should not be viewed as an insurmountable obstacle.

Getting started is associated with marketing. The question to answer is: Where do people live who will enroll their children in this program. Can the children walk to tennis, must they be transported, or must tennis go to the children. People at the local school board administrative offices, recreation departments, and the chamber of commerce have answers to these questions.

Staff

The second requirement is staff to teach. Facility owners and managers can hire and may train instructors. Consideration must be given to how many people are needed. Programs for young children, including Munchkin Tennis programs, operate with a very low student-teacher ratio. It is common to have one qualified instructor for every four to eight children. This results in combinations of four adults and high school students per court with a single court accommodating up to 16 Munchkins.

The nature of this age group is that they need one-on-one assistance for certain tennis activities like hitting forehands and backhands. Yet one person can conduct movement education activities, relay races and games like Musical Chairs for up to 30 children. The nature of your program determines your staff requirements.

The axiom that successful businesses follow to reduce turnover and cost while improving performance is "train and retain." Gregg Presuto has delivered Early Child Development Munchkin Tennis clinics nationally and internationally for the USPTR and the Tennis University.

Having a facility that can adapt to various aspects of Munchkin Tennis can enhance the quality of the program.

Facility

The next agenda item for consideration is either the facility or the plan. Staff members who have a facility can scan this part and go right to the planning process.

There are two attractive features of Munchkin Tennis. First, up to 16 youngsters can use one court. Second, preschool youngsters can participate in tennis with their parents when older students are in school. This yields greater facility utilization, and revenue.

Parent-instructors without a home base must pay particular attention to the facility question. Where will Munchkin Tennis be conducted? Either find a facility or be creative. For people without tennis facilities, churches, dance studios, day-care centers and gymnastic centers offer suitable space for lessons. Off-season ice rinks make fine Munchkin Tennis centers.

The nature of young children makes it possible to conduct Munchkin Tennis without courts. Ropes, portable nets and benches allow parents, teachers and recreation leaders to conduct programs in a variety of indoor or outdoor spaces. Gymnasiums, basketball courts, playgrounds, spare rooms, parking lots, church fellowship halls, preschool play spaces, dance studios, roller rinks, gymnastic centers and lawns offer unobstructed "court" space suitable for Munchkin Tennis. John Weil, Cincinnati tennis instructor, painted tennis court lines on the floor and set up a net in a small under-used exercise room. Parents without facilities or with inadequate facilities are limited only by their own ingenuity.

Planning

Planning is the third item on the agenda of concerns. Planning programs must be resolved first when new facility construction or renovation is considered. On the other hand, when facility questions are not an issue, the planning process starts with known parameters.

Planning is a revolving and continual three-step process. It

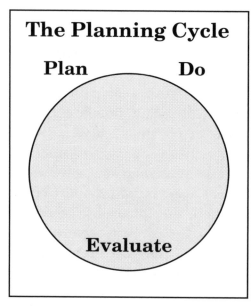

The Planning Cycle

Plan   **Do**

Evaluate

involves planning, doing, evaluation and replanning. It can be done formally or informally.

The purpose of planning is to determine the type of program desired. For young children, Munchkin Tennis should include a rich variety of activities and games with a minimum of instructional time, talk and lectures.

The dominant philosophy of Munchkin Tennis is to have fun learning tennis activities and games. The objective or end result of instruction is that young children be able to hit the ball consistently over the net, play games, and have fun. However, no specific plan is recommended in Munchkin Tennis. Develop your own system by answering these seven basic questions:

Proper planning is essential if there is a large group of Munchkin Tennis participants.

Who • What • When • Where • Why • How • How much

Who: Staff name(s) including a parent-director or coordinator.

What: Munchkin Tennis for ages nine and under; further age divisions that anticipated enrollment will permit, type of activities and games, special themes

When: Make a calendar; 30 to 60 minute sessions, number of times per week; times offered; what days during what weeks of the year.

Where: Inside or outside; number of courts available; which courts are available for Munchkin Tennis; other space available; space at other locations.

Why: Serve the community; fun for kids; develop future tennis players and future customers; generate revenue.

How: Children walk in; parents transport children to the center; staff go to other facilities such as day care centers, parks and schools; center provides vans or buses to bring Munchkins to the center.

How much: Income – Expenses = Profit. Cost of rackets and balls used or given to children, nets and other equipment, instructional fees, court time, t-shirts and snacks when provided. Determine your costs for space, travel and equipment. Then add your fee. Set a trail registration fee for each student. Estimate the number of students who will enroll. The bottom line is your profit.

Reduced-size equipment

The best equipment for Munchkin Tennis includes small rackets, a variety of soft and slow bounce balls, and short nets. Reduced-size equipment, along with good leadership, assures the success of young children in group lessons.

There is no prescribed equipment for Munchkin Tennis. That is, there are many ways to teach tennis to young children. Hence there is no specific equipment to be purchased. The rule of thumb

---

**Early Child Development
Munchkin Tennis Clinic
by Gregg Presuto**

Session One
Introduction to Munchkin Tennis
Introduction to a lesson plan
On court with the Munchkins
      Theme: Stroke production, Munchkin drills
Lesson review. Questions and Answers

Session Two
Introduction to a lesson plan
On court with Munchkins
      Theme: Munchkin Games
Lesson Review. Questions and Answers

Session Three
Discussion of Munchkin teaching philosophy
Psychological aspects of teaching Munchkins
      Relating to Munchkins; Personality types
      Maintaining attention; Reward systems
Teaching aids, Video tapes, On court use
More Munchkin contests and games
Munchkin Future
      Financial aspects
Review
Questions and Final Comments

---

is to simply make everything fit the children in size, weight, time and speed or slowness of movement. The slower the better.

The following equipment can be found in most USTA, physical education and recreation catalogs. Discount houses stock some of these items but they may not withstand heavy use. As a rule, when items cost a little more, they are of superior quality and withstand heavy use with true performance.

Rackets. Many companies like HEAD Sports produce small, short or junior rackets. They are available in several lengths at prices often under $25.00.

Other rackets can be used for tennis activities and games including wooden paddles, plastic rackets found in most discount houses, plus racquetball and badminton rackets.

Very light rackets can be made by slipping stockings over paddle-shaped clothes hangers. Balloons make perfect balls, inside and outside, but not on windy days.

Small, light homemade paddles with rounded handles can be made in wood shops by crafty tennis players and parents. This helps reduce the cost of tennis, particularly if used rackets are donated and modified.

Anneke Jelsma-de Jong, Dutch tennis pro, uses paddles made with gloves tacked or glued to round boards. See Chapter 9, page 250. It teaches children to use both hands, both sides of the body. She said: "It is easy to learn tennis when the ball is near the hand."

Other commercial products similar to round boards are hand paddles used in swim training. They are available in several sizes and cost about $5.00 a pair.

Short nets. Short nets can be made of ropes or benches. Commercially manufactured short nets are also available. Sportime, a catalog distributor, sells two different short net and post systems. Costs range between $100 and $450.00. Their address is: Sportime, One Sportime Way, Atlanta GA 30340 or telephone 800 283-5700.

For nets in Germany, contact Gerhard Glasbrenner, President of the Southern Section of the German Tennis Teachers Association—VDT—and a USPTR member. His address is Reutenerstrasse 54, 88142 Lindau-Wasserburg. The phone number is 08382 1060 and the fax number is 08382 1026.

Other "nets" for young children can be obstacles over which to hit. From low to high, they are: court line, chalk line, tape line, rope or jump rope, towels, markers, racket on end, bench, chair, ball hopper, short net, regular net, players with rackets, players with brooms, elevated ropes on poles, and court fences.

Slow bounce tennis balls. New tennis balls are very bouncy and difficult for young children to track and hit. Old tennis balls that have lost some of their bounce are quite good for Munchkin Tennis.

Slow bounce tennis balls are available. Products include the Tretorn ST and the JCS 100 (short court) and JCS 135 (full court). The latter is a West German product sold in the USA through Sportime.

Many types of sponge, foam, fleece, rubber, and plastic balls are available in tennis ball size, about 2 5/8" in diameter. They can be found in many physical education and recreation catalogs and discount stores. Costs range from $1.50 to over $5.00 each.

In addition to tennis balls, other balls can be used to learn hand-eye coordination and ball sense. They include playground balls, basketballs, soccer balls, volleyballs, and beach balls.

Costs start at about $10.00 for those that retain their shape and texture with heavy use on rough surfaces. Mesh ball sacks costing $5.00 to $10.00 are available for carrying and storage. Balloons also make good slow moving "tennis balls."

Other teaching aids. Teaching aids make learning to play tennis easier and more fun. They include ball hoppers, tennis tubes, jump ropes, ball carts, cones or markers.

U.S.A. Special Events Planning Calendar

New Year's Day	Flag Day
M. L. King Birthday	Father's Day
NFL Super Bowl	First Day of Summer
Lincoln's Birthday	Canada Day
President's Day	Independence Day
Washington's Birthday	Olympics
Groundhog Day	Labor Day
St. Valentine's Day	First Day of Autumn
St. Patrick's Day	Yom Kippur
First Day of Spring	Columbus Day
Easter	World Series
NBA Playoffs	Halloween
Stanley Cup Playoff	Election Day
Mother's Day	Veteran's Day
Victoria Day	Thanksgiving
Memorial Day	First Day of Winter
Wimbledon	Christmas

Ball machines provide a consistent way to feed balls to children while working near the children or helping others. When using regular ball machines with young children, the force of delivery must be reduced to the slowest speed. Balls that take two low bounces, rather than one high bounce, are easy for them to track and hit.

Serves-U-Right is an electric 30-ball machine well suited to Munchkin Tennis. It can be ordered through Stroke Master. The address is P.O. Box 822870, Dallas, TX 75382. The phone number is 1-800-527-7187.

Targets are used in many instructional programs for young children. They can be fixed to walls, curtains, nets and fences or placed at strategic locations on the court. They provide youngsters with a point of aim, an end.

Remember, they will forget what was said about skill. Targets help children make specific movements with cues like, "Get the ball

all the way into the backcourt target on the fly." When successful, in all probability, they will execute many points of skill properly, and it will be done without dull lectures.

The Targetmaxxer target trainer is available from GRT, Inc. Please write to them at 5600 Oakbrook Parkway, Suite 120, Norcross, GA 30093 or call 800-635-5042.

Other targets include: areas of the court, court lines, hula hoops, jump ropes laid out in squares and triangles, two square and four square courts, hop scotch courts, buckets, boxes, and towels. Chalk can be used to make lines on playing surfaces.

Many instructors use sport and holiday themes in lessons to build enthusiasm. Children can help cut out craft paper decorations and targets. The list on page 285 serves as a handy reminder. Mark them on your Munchkin Tennis calendar each year.

Making it work for you

Business tips. Tennis people who were interviewed for Munchkin Tennis provided a number of "helpful business tips." When followed, they help ensure that objectives are accomplished and programs are successful.

- Self-motivated people make programs successful. There is no substitute for good people.
- Work at Munchkin Tennis, innovate and communicate with the public.
- Be flexible and adaptable, particularly when getting started.
- Use reduced-size equipment for young children: rackets, balls and nets.
- Sell small rackets in the facility or out of your car or van.
- Be prepared to bring in qualified assistants when the program grows. Train staff members and use teenagers who are familiar with or have been through the program.
- Have a first aid kit available at every session.
- Provide regular water and shade breaks on hot and humid days outside.

- Ask parents or other staff to help in bathrooms, particularly for children not in school.
- Learn from others who work with small children.
- Conduct special events to build and maintain enthusiasm among the participants.
- Keep the children active.
- Develop a daily format or regimen so youngsters learn what to expect.
- Use tennis activities and games and make it look like real tennis.
- Evaluate the performance of children with parents.
- Get parents involved as aids and boosters.
- Play with the children and have fun with them.
- Help them hit the ball, keep the ball between the lines and have fun.

Generate clients and revenue. Program leaders want stability. This allows parents, instructors, owners and managers to concentrate on running tennis programs rather than prospecting for new registration fees to pay the bills. To do this, operate the program like a business so that it pays for itself. Here are recommendations that many sport operations follow.
- Be prepared to tell about the program to community groups.
- Establish tennis for young children as a non-profit corporation and then network with other youth serving agencies in the community.
- Ask a local company or companies to sponsor a short video that describes the program and make it available upon request for all functions.
- Assemble a catalog or wish list with prices of items needed for the program.
- Generate revenue by developing a sales package that shows how a program sponsorship will generate a return on investment or positive public image for potential sponsors.

Marketing and Advertising

Marketing is locating customers. Advertising is telling them about your products and services and why they need them. Here are ways people who run tennis programs for young children have "sold" the community on their services.

- Word of mouth. Ask other parents and children to tell a friend, or bring a friend.
- Post sign-up sheets at entrances to your facility.
- Place posters in busy entrances and local stores.
- Make the logo and characters associated with the program cute. See the camera ready art work on the following page. It can be used for posters, brochures, shirts and caps.
- Print brochures and distribute them through classes, over the counter, through the club, and in area stores.
- Announce starting dates in the free calendar section of the local newspapers.
- Send direct mail flyers to known customers.
- Distribute a quarterly newsletter over the counter and by direct mail to current customers. Hand it out at clinics and talks.
- Offer seasonal or monthly flat fee group lesson rates.
- Conduct play days and free tennis clinics in schools, for Scouts, on Saturday mornings or Sunday afternoons, and other youth groups.
- Conduct video days where play is taped or skills are corrected.
- Do a radio show.
- Write a column for the weekly or daily newspaper.
- Send public service announcements to the local media about your special event and ask them to do a story.
- Develop a team tennis concept that develops players for the local high school.

Preparing parents

If you have decided to become more involved with teaching tennis to groups of preschoolers and other Munchkins, the tables may be reversed. You, the parent/instructor, must be prepared to explain your goals, methods and skills to other parents. As you know, tennis can mean much more than providing a small racket, three new tennis balls and court shoes. Some parents view lessons as the first step on the way to tournament tennis and lucrative professional careers.

Tennis instructors who were interviewed about their tennis program for young children reported great cooperation and support from parents in what they were doing for their children. This was by design. They also had frank discussions with highly competitive parents. The latter tended not to remain with these programs beyond one series of lessons. They were usually satisfied with nothing less than traditional instruction and world class performance from their children. This occurred despite the good feelings their children expressed for Munchkin-type programs.

Comments about parents were typical of those expressed by Anneke Jelsma-de Jong of Holland, developer of Easy Tennis. She said: "I explain the program to parents in advance. They understand the concept and accept it for their children."

This is not to say there were no problems. Parents questioned what certain activities had to do with tennis, or how rapidly their children were progressing. Sometimes parents played at home or at the court with full sized equipment that interfered with what they were learning in class. Parents might expect more from their children than they were capable of doing, as one instructor explained.

Those interviewed did one thing in common that made life easier for everyone. They helped parents understand tennis for young children. Parents were given an orientation to the program or handouts at registration. Orientation included explanations of the goals and purposes of the program. Then, parents knew what to expect in advance, and were cooperative from the start. Parents who were told about their child's tennis program in advance, who later raised questions, were also more understanding and cooperative.

Parents disagreed on what they expected from tennis for their young children. Some instructors felt parents wanted the activities and games to be very much like real tennis. In contrast to this, Marceil Whitney, preschool tennis instructor, told what one parent wrote to her. "We continue to come back because our kids love it. They are having fun, and I do not care if they are learning real tennis."

Some parents want to play tennis with their young children. Their inclination might be to run them through prolonged drills, particularly if they have had tennis lessons themselves.

Parent/instructors can provide parents with more appropriate alternatives. During orientation, demonstrate games and activities from your program that they can "play" with their children. Explain how they should be patient and allow children to develop at their own pace.

It is important to explain that patience means parents should realize their children will progress at "their own" pace. They may be nine to 11 years of age before they can play tennis games over the net in the service courts or rally consistently from the baseline. This, of course, depends on the amount of time children spend on the court and how much fun they are having. Even then, the task of parents is to play the ball to the child, not hit winners.

Conduct short mini-clinics at the end of class periodically for parents. Show them good activities to do with their children and how to keep them playful, fun.

There are several activities and games that are particularly good games for parents and children. They can be played at home or on a court and include: Alley Rally, Bounce ball off a wall, Crazy Catches, Follow The Leader, Golf Tennis, Dizzy Lizzy, Hit the ball to a parent from an easy toss, Hot Potato, and Ups & Downs.

Sally Hutslar, former collegiate player and coach, started her daughter Jo Ellen in tennis as a preschooler using a variety of plastic rackets and soft balls. She graduated to an old racquetball racket and then a junior racket. Sally and Jo Ellen, with husband Jack, played a three-person game for several years. Jo Ellen would stand between Sally and husband Jack. Sally tossed the ball to Jo Ellen, attempting to put the ball where she swung. Jo Ellen would hit the ball to Mom and Dad would catch the misses. They did it in the driveway and one side of a tennis court. As Jo Ellen grew, they stood on each side of the net, and then moved back to the service line. Jo Ellen, at age 9, could rally baseline to baseline with parents taking turns hitting and retrieving stray balls. At age 10, she played full court tennis against older children. At age 14, she played number three singles and number two doubles on a small high school tennis team. She still enjoys a variety of tennis games — including Tiny Tennis played in the service court. Her parents know that she can become a much better high school player. They also know that the commitment to work hard and really improve will have to be her decision.

When parents register children for tennis, tell them about the program in advance, answer their questions, and show them what they can do with their children. It will produce more cooperative attitudes and understanding parents. Parents who remain dissatisfied may wish to enroll their children in more formal private and semi-private lessons.

Tennis consumer catalogs offer starter sets for children ages nine and under. They include mini rackets (4" grip, a 12' X 30" net, and foam balls). Discount stores sell plastic tennis sets that can be used inside or outside. Complete tennis sets will enable parents to play with their children at home.

Summary

A trainer in the business world said that "success comes from doing ordinary things an extraordinary number of times." The ordinary things that must be done over and over to have successful programs for young children are planning lessons, recruiting children, training staff and parents, taking care of facilities, using reduced-size equipment so children can be successful, and keeping parents informed.

Highly visible college and professional sport programs and their stars command a great deal of attention from the media and sponsors. Programs for children "go begging" in comparison. As a rule, there are no short cuts in developing successful programs for children. But then, what is good that comes easy.

The purpose of Munchkin Tennis is to provide parents, some of whom may become tennis instructors, with insight into the nature of young children and how they learn. The primary focus of Munchkin Tennis is activities and games. It offers many ways to conduct tennis in an enjoyable, yet educational way.

The activities and games are presented in a progression. The progression begins in Chapter 4 with an explanation of tennis skills young children can learn. In Chapter 5, tennis activity begins with movement education, first without and then with tennis racket and ball. Next, in Chapter 6, low organized games provide easy and enjoyable tennis action. Lead-up games follow in Chapter 7. Most children see how similar lead-up games are to real tennis. Chapter 8, the last of four chapters on skill, presents the Graduated Tennis Method.

The last two chapters of Munchkin Tennis describe several current tennis programs for young children. The book ends with many practical suggestions to help instructors, managers and owners design and develop sound tennis programs for young children.

The philosophy of Munchkin Tennis is simple. It is to help young children learn how to keep the ball on the court between the lines, play a variety of tennis games, and have fun.

About the author of Munchkin Tennis

Dr. Jack Hutslar is a nationally known youth sport specialist, writer, lecturer, and consultant. He has worked in education and sports all of his life. Dr. Jack is the author of BEYOND X's and O's, a complete how to . . . manual for parents who coach, and coaches who are not trained teachers. Hutslar writes and edits Sport Scene; researched and wrote the YABA Coaches' Manual: Beginning Bowling for the Young American Bowling Alliance and designed the training program provided for all YABA coaches. He was the featured coach in the Official Pop Warner Football Video Handbook and a 1988 YABA pilot video for teachers. He is the education consultant to Youth Basketball of America. Hutslar has produced educational materials for organizations serving well over one million youngsters annually. He is a "sport junkie" who includes tennis, baseball and running among his favorite sport activities.

Bibliography

The following sources provide information for parents, teachers and youth leaders who want to teach tennis to their own children and other children in private and community youth sport programs.

Bennett, John P. and Artie Kamiya. *Fitness and Fun*. Durham NC: The Great Activities Publishing Company, 1986, 140 pp. Filled with practical fitness activities using teaching stations that can be incorporated into tennis, or other sport programs.

Brown, Eugene W. and Crystal F. Branta (eds). *Competitive Sports for Children and Youth: An overview of research and issues*. Champaign: Human Kinetics Books, 1988, 314 pp. Recent research findings about children.

Carlyle, Sue. *Move To Learn*. Norfolk VA: Bleecker Street Publishing Corporation, 1983, 61 pp. $8.95. Movement, rope and ball activities that young children love to do.

Cassidy, John and B. C. Rimbeaux. *Juggling for the Complete Klutz*, 3rd ed. Palo Alto: Klutz Press, 1988, 82 pp. Step by step procedures.

Christina, Robert W. and Daniel M. Corcos. *Coaches Guide To Teaching Sport Skills*. Champaign: Human Kinetics Publishers, Inc., 1988, 168 pp. General guide for anyone working with young children to school teams.

Cratty, Bryant J. *Active Learning*, 2nd ed. Englewood Cliffs: Prentice-Hall, Inc., 1985, 163 pp. Provides active games for learning to calm down, spatial concepts, remembering, math, and language arts.

Dougherty, Neil J. and Diane Bonanno. *Contemporary Approaches to the Teaching of Physical Education*. Scottsdale AZ: Gorsuch Scarisbrick, Publishers, 1987, 261 pp. Practical ways to improve teaching skills, particularly with young children.

Figelman, Alan R. and Patrick Young. *Keeping Young Athletes Healthy*. New York: Fireside Books, 1991. 319 pp., $9.95. What every parent and volunteer coach should know.

Glover, Bob and Jack Shepherd. *The Family Fitness Handbook*. New York: Penguin Books, 1989, 417 pp., $9.95. Parent and child fitness fun, aerobic endurance, strength and flexibility, sports programs, nutrition, stress and safety.

Graham, George and others. *Children Moving*. Palo Alto: Mayfield Publishing Company, 1980, 503 pp. $20.95. Text book for elementary school physical education teachers. Contains many games divided into pre-control, control, utilization and proficiency levels with section on racket skills.

Hutslar, Jack. *Beyond X's and O's: What generic parents can learn about generic kids and all of the sports they play*. Welcome NC: Wooten, 1985, 231 pp. $8.95. Complete how to . . . coaching guide for parents, teachers, and youth coaches who want their kids to learn more, play safely and have more fun. Available by sending $10.45 to NAYSI, 4985 Oak Garden Drive, Kernersville NC 27284.

Hutslar, Jack. *The USPTR Manual of Munchkin Tennis. Instructor's Manual, Volume 9*. Hilton Head Island, SC: United States Professional Tennis Registry, 1989, 332 pp. $20.00. How to teach tennis to children age nine and younger with hundreds of games to make it more fun

Kraemer, William J. and Steven J. Fleck. *Strength Training for Young Athletes*. Champaign: Human Kinetics Publishers, 1993, 214 pp., $16.95. Includes over 100 safe exercises for 18 muscle groups and 16 sports.

Magill, Richard A. *Motor Learning: Concepts and applications*, 2nd ed. Dubuque: Wm. C. Brown Publishers, 1985, 451 pp. Scientific basis of human movement written in understandable terms.

Martens, Rainer and others. *Coaching Young Athletes*. Champaign: Human Kinetics Publishers, Inc., 1981, 224 pp. $12.00. Covers many topics for coaches related to safe programs for children.

McInally, Pat. *Moms & Dads - Kids & Sports*. New York: Macmillan Publishing Company, 1988, 238 pp., $14.95. General information about children in sport with specific sports considered.

Micheli, Lyle J. Sportswise: *An essential guide for young athletes, parents and coaches.* Boston: Houghton Mifflin, 1990, 300 pp., $19.95. Expert advise on preventing injuries, building health fitness, improving sports programs and more.

Morris, G. S. Don and Jim Stiehl. *Changing Kids' Games.* Champaign: Human Kinetics Books, 1989, 144 pp. $10.00. All about planning, designing and presenting games, plus a bunch of games.

NAYSI Resource List. Send stamped self-addressed envelope to NAYSI Resource List, 4985 Oak Garden Drive, Kernersville NC 27284. Receive free list of book and other resources for people who work with young children in sport, recreation, education, fitness and health.

Rookie Coaches Tennis Guide. Champaign: Leisure Press, 191, 76 pp., $8.95. Teaching, coaching and tennis skills that adults should know when working with children.

Rotella, Robert J. and Linda K. Bunker. *Parenting Your Superstar: How to help your child get the most out of sports.* Champaign: Leisure Press, 1987, 238 pp. Good book for parents who want to do what is best for their child.

Seefeldt, Vern and Paul Vogel. *The Value of Physical Activity.* Reston VA: AAHPERD, 1986, 39 pp. Research base of the objectives for physical activity.

Seefeldt, Vern (ed). *Handbook For Youth Sports Coaches.* Reston VA: AAHPERD, 1987, 379 pp., $14.95 Latest book by AAHPERD Youth Sport Coalition for coaches.

Singer, Robert N. *Sustaining Motivation in Sport.* Tallahassee: Consultants International, Inc., 1984, 104 pp. Numerous ways to motivate.

Smoll, Frank L, Richard A. Magill and Michael J. Ash. *Children in Sport* (3rd ed). Champaign: Human Kinetics Publishers, Inc., 1988, 348 pp. Recent research findings.

Sport Scene: focus on youth programs. Dr. Jack Hutslar, editor and publisher. $16 per year. c/o North American Youth Sport Institute, 4985 Oak Garden Drive, Kernersville NC 27284.

Practical program ideas, research summaries, coaching tips, book reviews and commentaries about all kinds of sport activities for children.

Torbert, Marianne. *Follow Me.* Englewood Cliffs: Prentice-Hall, Inc., 1980, 214 pp., $6.95. Book of games for children with goals such as social interaction, attention, creativity and emotional control.

USPTR Tennis Training Manual, Volume 1, United States Professional Tennis Registry, P. O. Box 4739, Hilton Head Island, SC 29938. Skills, fundamentals and progressions that can be adapted for youngsters.

Weiss, Maureen R. and Daniel Gould, (eds). *Sport for Children and Youths.* Champaign: Human Kinetics Publishers, Inc., 1986, 284 pp. Commentaries and research findings from many theoretical points of view.

Winter, Gillian. *A Child Is Not A Little Adults: Modified approaches to sport for Australian children* (2nd ed.), Hobart: Tasmanian State Schools Sports Council, 1983, 156 pp., $10.95. General information with section on tennis.

INDEX

Activity Time, 22

Advertising, 288

Arousal, 28

Ball machines, 270

Be Positive, 24-29

Bibliography, 295-298

Bill of Rights for Young Athletes, 54

Brown, Jim, 267-271

    Tennis Buddies, 267-271

Children, 277, 9-17

    characteristics, 10, 15

    not miniature adults, 9

    success with, 48

Cosgrove, Colleen, 60, 261-264

    Pee Wee, 60, 261-264

Dahlgren, Leif, 252-253

    Mini-Tennis, 252-253

Discipline, 16

    a plan, 34

Disruptive children, 32

Early Childhood Development Clinic, 282

Equipment, 281-286

Etiquette, 49

Expect success, 26

Facilities, 279

Formations, action, 35-38

Graduated Tennis Method, 241-247

    method, 242

    skills, 247

    steps, 242

Hand-eye coordination, 12-14
Hutslar, Jack, 272-274, 294
        Tiny Tennis, 272-274
Hutslar, Sally, 291-292
Instructional Time, 22
Jelsma-de Jong, Anneke, 250-252
        Easy Tennis, 250-252
        wooden paddles, 250-252
Leadership, 43
Low organized games, 79-214
Making it work for you, 286
Management Time, 22
Marketing, 288
        and advertising, 288
Model, 2,
        Children + Tennis = Fun, 2, 43
        people, 3
        philosophy, 5
        tennis, the sport, 4
Modeling, 26
Motivation, 27
Munchkin Tennis,
        camera ready art, 289
        Easy Tennis, 250-252
        fundamental movements, 59
        games, 79-215, 219-238
        goals, 5-7, 51-52
        juggling, 63-65
        Mini-Tennis, 252-253
        model, 2, 4
        movement education, 57-63
        Pee Wee, 261-264
        Preschool, 264-267
        philosophy, 5

Phillips, Teresa, 258-260
Presuto, Gregg, 253-258
starting, 277
Skills Checklist, 55
start lessons, 60
Tennis Buddies, 267-272
Tennis Tasks, 66-78
Tiny Tennis, 273-275
NAYSI Teacher Self-help Checklist, 40-41
Objectives, 5-7, 50-52
game, 52
individual tennis, 51
physiological, 52
social, 51
Parents
preparing, 290-292
orientation, 290
People, 3
Phillips, Teresa, 258-260
format, 259
Planned ignoring, 33
Planning, 279
Playfulness, 19
Positive reinforcement, 25
Presuto, Gregg, 35, 253-258
Psychology
practical tips, 29-35
Punishment, 33
Rackets, 283
Re-direction, 34
Reduced size equipment, 281-284
Safety, 47
Self-concept, 28
Short nets, 283
Shy children, 31

Skills
    for players, 44
    for parents, 44
Slow bounce tennis balls, 284
Spacial relations, 13-14
Special events calendar, 285
Staff, 277
Standing In Line Time, 23
Success, 26
Tagging, 80
Take A.I.M. on Time, 21-24
Targets, 285-286
Teaching
    aids, 284
    formations, action, 35-38
    major points, 46
    participation or elimination, 80
    self-help, 40-41
    stations, 38-39
    start lessons, 60
    success, 48
    winning and losing, 81
Tennis
    activities, 57-78
    lead up games, 217-239
    low organized games, 79-214
    Munchkin, 253-258
    Graduated Tennis Method, 241-247
    tasks, 66-78
    the sport, 4
Token economy, 33
Tracking, 14
Transfer of training, 11
    positive, 12
Van der Meer, Dennis, 2, 241

Weil, John, 27, 45, 279
Whitney, Marceil, 264-267
        Preschool, 264-267
Who, what, when, where, why, how, how much, 281
Wooden paddles, 2, 250-252

The works of Jack Hutslar,
North American Youth Sport Institute

Munchkin Tennis, United States Professional Tennis Registry (1993)

How To Conduct Successful Tournaments: Play, profit and people, Youth Basketball of America (1993)

The USPTR Manual of Munchkin Tennis, United States Professional Tennis Registry (1988)

YABA Coaching Manual: Beginning Bowling, Young American Bowling Alliance (1987)

The Official Pop Warner Football Video Handbook, Pop Warner Little Scholars (1987)

Beyond X's and O's: What generic parents can learn about generic kids and all of the sports they play, North American Youth Sport Institute (1985)